100

Ar

19

the 19th annual blackbook AR100 awards show

Design
Elements

{DETERMINATION}	DN_	DE_	{DESIGN}
{TONE}	TO_	HE_	{PHOTOGRAPHY}
{ILLUSTRATION}	IL_	CO_	{COLOR}
{INTUITION}	IN_	TE_	{TEXTURE}
{SOUL}	SO_	GU_	{GUTS}

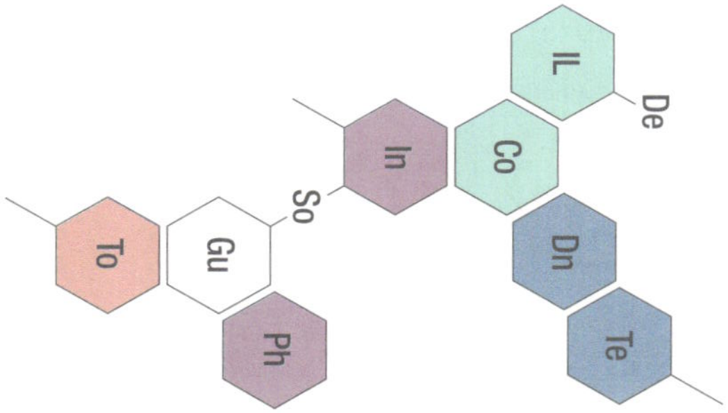

Creating the right reaction in the eyes and minds of corporate clients and their annual report audiences is part art and part science, part chemistry and part alchemy. Always challenging, dealing as it must with so many variables-- with so many solid, liquid, and gaseous materials with the numbers, the messages, the politics.

Of course, there are fundamental formulas one can follow which will produce a practical book with predictable results. However, it's the artistry, "the alchemy," if you will, with the interaction of intangibles like insight and inspiration, which takes the average annual experiment to a higher level. These elements yield something far more interesting and arresting, far more dynamic and distinctive than an expression produced from a simple formula. So how does this happen? It's all about combining the right elements ñ in the right way, from the designer and writer, to the photographer and printer, to the story and the paper it's printed on, all crystallizing and harmonizing their focus. Catalyzing the entire process with kinetic thinking and creative approaches in the end will ignite those "a-ha" moments, those atomic and subatomic flashes of awareness and interest, messages and impressions you want for each person reading that report.

The equation works, for rocket and non-rocket scientists alike.

What's the litmus test? Producing an annual which transforms and transmutes the typical properties of printed words, images and pages into the precious substance from which a company's soul and success are made.

Reports formed from exceptional and attainable mixtures of imagination, skill, and feverish exploration of those featured in this year's AR100.

THE CHEMISTRY
(AND ALCHEMY)
OF GOOD DESIGN

colin goedecke

19

no.

THE 19TH ANNUAL BLACK BOOK
AR100 AWARD SHOW

AR100
Publisher
assaf ran
dag media

President
ted rubin

Vice President & Sales Manager
magi lipson

Vice President
andreas panagopoulos

AR100 Project Manager
anne eaton

Assistant AR100 Project Manager
alexandra pratt

PRODUCTION
Production Manager
jason sturdevant

Graphic Designer
vicky lau

CIRCULATION/LISTINGS
Senior Listings Coordinator
desiree ambrose

WEBSITE
Multimedia Manager
josephine hu

Web sales/customer service
tom mallory

ACCOUNTING
Senior accounting/ receivables
farida dhanji

Bookeeper
cindy kong

EXECUTIVE ASSISTANT
winona cobb

MARKETING CONSULTANTS
(AR100) richard perkin

(PHOTOGRAPHY)
NORTHEAST & INTERNATIONAL erica sturdevant

SOUTH karen nathan

WEST magi lipson

(ILLUSTRATION) adrian johnson

(CREATIVE INDUSTRY DIRECTORY & AR100)
abi laoshe
noah david simon
andrew ellinghaus
eran evron
anwar ghazal
shimrit shoshan

MARKETING CONSULTANTS
(ON-LINE PORTFOLIOS) tom mallory

SALES ADMINISTRATION maggie kenny

BOOK CONCEPT AND DESIGN
kurt finkbeiner / steve ferrari
graphic expression inc.
www.tgenyc.com
212 725 8080

CONCEPTUAL WRITING
colin goedecke
www.tenowls.com

PAPER
sappi fine paper
225 franklin street
boston ma 02110
p: 800 822 idea
p: 617 423 7300
f: 617 423 5491
ar100 awards show book
printed on sappi fine paper
100 lb/270 gsm gloss cover
100 lb/148 gsm dull text
120 lb/325 gsm dull cover

JUDGES PORTRAITS
lou bopp
www.loubopp.com
p: 212 665 6400

DISTRIBUTION
black book ar100 award show book is distributed in the u.s. and canada by the black book.

OUTSIDE DISTRIBUTION
AVA Publishing sa
sales / editorial office
56a chapel road
worthing west sussex BN11 1DQ
united kingdom
p: 44 1903 204455
f: 44 1903 204455

BLACKBOOK
740 broadway
suite 202
new york, ny 10003
p: 212 979 6700
f: 212 673 4321
www.blackbook.com
a subsidiary of Dag media
125-10 queens boulevard
suite 14
kew gardens, ny 11415
p: 718 520 1000
f: 718 793 2522

ISBN 0-942454-91-X
ISNN 1093-6521

Judges

AR 100

AT_ {ANNA TAN}
DW_ {DAVID STOYAN WOOTERS}
DM_ {DEAN MARTIN}
KH_ {KENT HUNTER}

Anna Tan is a senior designer at The Corporate Agenda, a creative agency based in New York City. Corporate Agenda specializes in producing integrated and innovative communications for clients around the world. A premium on ideas and a dedication to achieving high production values is easily said but difficult to achieve. Anna's ability to do just this explains why she is one of the founding members of the team and is so greatly valued by clients and colleagues alike. An alumnus of the Rochester Institute of Technology, Anna learned her trade in a number of well-respected design firms such as Emerson Wajdowicz Studios, Addison, Red Sky/Belk Mignogna Associates and The Corporate Agenda.

Anna's work is as diverse as the client list: MasterCard, Procter & Gamble, The Estee Lauder Companies, Children's Television Workshop, Eastman Kodak Company, Turner Construction, Nabisco, and NYCE. Impressive names and equally impressive work. Work that's been recognized with accolades and awards including - Graphis, Black Book AR100, The Society of Publication Design, Mercury, ARC Awards, and The New York Festivals.

Despite her hectic schedule, Anna continues to find time to enjoy life with her family. The spur of the moment trip to Hawaii, a growing photography collection and a seemingly grueling yoga schedule ensure that life is never predictably designed.

ANNA TAN

the corporate agenda

David Stoyan Wooters is Principal and Creative Director of the Costa Mesa, California-based graphic design firm Stoyan Design. Born and raised in Southern California, David is an alumnus of Cal State Long Beach. Shortly after graduating in 1985, David founded Stoyan Design and since then the firm has grown to become one of the most respected multi-disciplined corporate design agencies in the country, with a body of work that includes annual reports, branding, identity systems, advertising, catalogs, multimedia and web site design.

The culture of Stoyan Design is founded on the belief that every project must be driven by a strong central message, and every aspect of the project must convey and reinforce that message. By staying true to its culture, the firm's work has been recognized by many national and multi-national competitions and publications, including Graphis Annual Report, Communication Arts, the Mead Annual Report Show, the New York Art Directors Club, the Art Directors Club of Los Angeles, the Sappi Design Awards Show, Print Magazine and the AR100 Award Show.

In the annual report arena, Stoyan Design has been fortunate to work with a very diverse mix of companies who are accepting of unique approaches and understand the power of a compelling annual report. David's open minded approach to problem-solving allows for a creative atmosphere, where any idea can be shared and explored. A collaborative effort among all staff members ensure quality results for each project delivered. Sometimes the process of finding just the right corporate message to be conveyed in an annual report can be a difficult task, yet it is always worthwhile. Sharpening a corporate message that resonates within the company, throughout the industry and investor community is a priceless service that a good annual report design firm can provide and, in doing so, can solidify the future of the annual report itself.

DAVID STOYAN WOOTERS

stoyan design

Dean Martin is the Creative Director for Spencer Francey Peters, a top Canadian branding and design firm based in Toronto. He has extensive experience in corporate identity, brand strategy and print communication, including corporate identity work for Canada Trust, The Toronto Stock Exchange, Direct Energy, AGF Financial Services and Maple Leaf Foods. Other clients include Canada Post, Chase Manhattan Bank and Laura Secord Chocolates. In addition to his corporate background, Dean has worked with numerous cultural institutions, including the National Museums of Agriculture and Aviation, McMaster Museum of Art, Drabinsky Gallery and the Mercer Union Centre for Contemporary Art. In 1998 Dean co-designed a series of 10 postage stamps for Canada Post which celebrated historic canals of Canada. The set was the largest commission of the year and became an immediate hit with collectors.

Dean holds a Bachelor of Design degree from the Nova Scotia College of Art and Design and studied at the Cooper Union in New York City. His work has been recognized nationally and internationally by The Advertising and Design Club of Canada, Applied Arts Magazine, Graphis, HQ Magazine, and the Design Exchange, and has also appeared in such volumes as International Corporate Design and Symbols and Trademarks of Canada.

Dean has been invited to judge in many high profile design competitions, including the AR 100 and the Applied Arts Advertising and Design Awards. Before his appointment to Creative Director of SFP, he was a principal in the multi-disciplinary design studio Carey George Dean Martin.

DEAN MARTIN

SPENCER FRANCEY PETERS

Kent Hunter is the Executive Creative Director and Partner of Diversified Media Design, New York.

After designing and directing annual reports for almost twenty years at Frankfurt Balkind, Kent is now a partner in DMD New York, a communications consultancy integrating marketing, technology and creative expertise.

His work for corporations such as Time Warner, The Limited, Adobe, Sony, Goldman Sachs and Merrill Lynch has won many awards and is included in the Cooper-Hewitt National Design Museum's permanent collection. He has worked with The Getty, Japan Society and the Guggenheim Museum and is particularly interested in the convergence of cultures.

A past board member of AIGA New York, he frequently lectures, judges design shows and collects folk art, dice and the pieces of cardboard that come in Chinese take-out bags.

KENT HUNTER

Diversified Media Design

BEST OFs

TOP 10s

THE AR 100

INDEX

PHOTOGRAPHERS

INDEX

ILLUSTRATORS

DESIGN, PRINTER, PAPER and PUBLISHING

Design

Printer

Paper

Publishing

Stimulate your palette...introducing
Kromekote® Candy
Jenny
SMART
PAPERS

TALENT
RESOURCES

James Schnepf
262 375 2600
schnepfphoto.com

SCOTT WITTE ON LOCATION

AWARDS CA PRINT ADDY KODAK

scottwitte.com 414.345.9660

Lou Bōpp Photography
212-665-6400 • lou@loubopp.com • www.loubopp.com
represented by Elise Caputo • 212-725-0503

PORTRAITURE
CORPORATE
EDITORIAL
ADVERTISING
ON LOCATION

www.allemanphoto.com
323.906.0460

THOMAS MICHAEL
alleman

Kenneth Gabrielsen
Photography

212.741.6968
914.827.3970

www.gabrielsenphotography.com

The Drake

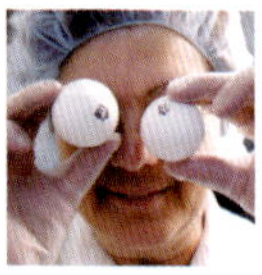

© Doug Knutson

Jim Karageorge

THE EXTRAORDINARY PEOPLE OF EXELIXIS, INC.

— 2003 EXELIXIS ANNUAL REPORT

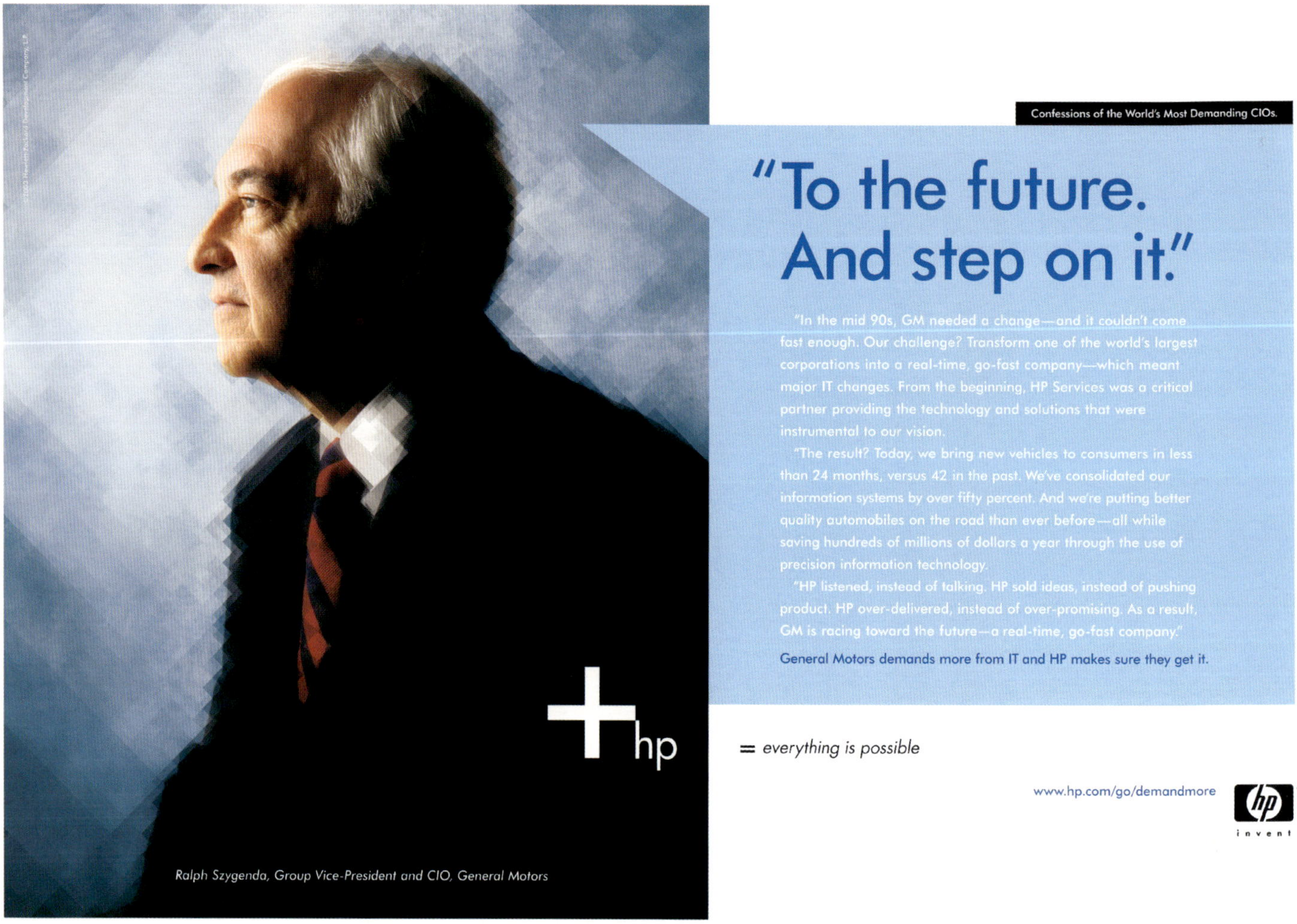
Confessions of the World's Most Demanding CIOs.
"To the future. And step on it."
"In the mid 90s, GM needed a change—and it couldn't come fast enough. Our challenge? Transform one of the world's largest corporations into a real-time, go-fast company—which meant major IT changes. From the beginning, HP Services was a critical partner providing the technology and solutions that were instrumental to our vision.
"The result? Today, we bring new vehicles to consumers in less than 24 months, versus 42 in the past. We've consolidated our information systems by over fifty percent. And we're putting better quality automobiles on the road than ever before—all while saving hundreds of millions of dollars a year through the use of precision information technology.
"HP listened, instead of talking. HP sold ideas, instead of pushing product. HP over-delivered, instead of over-promising. As a result, GM is racing toward the future—a real-time, go-fast company."
General Motors demands more from IT and HP makes sure they get it.
+ hp
= everything is possible
www.hp.com/go/demandmore
invent
Ralph Szygenda, Group Vice-President and CIO, General Motors

William Coupon

81 Nassau Street, Studio 2i
New York, New York 10038
212.406.6936

www.williamcoupon.com

Powell Design photographed for Business 2.0

Robert Schoen Photography

T 978.897.3242
W www.schoenphoto.com
E robert@schoenphoto.com

Rachel Pascazio, NewSouth Communications

Craig Bromley Photography

Clients Include: American Express, C.A.R.E., Coca-Cola, Delta,
Florida Power and Light, Forbes, Georgia–Pacific, Harper's and Queen,
IBM, Kimberly–Clark, Philips, Red Herring, Sheraton, Smart Money, Time and UPS.

See the portfolio at www.cbromley.com or call 404.881.0767

Mike Eskew, Chairman and CEO, UPS

Craig Bromley Photography

Clients Include: American Express, C.A.R.E., Coca-Cola, Delta,
Florida Power and Light, Forbes, Georgia–Pacific, Harper's and Queen,
IBM, Kimberly–Clark, Philips, Red Herring, Sheraton, Smart Money, Time and UPS.

See the portfolio at www.cbromley.com or call 404.881.0767

MEAT,

human emotions

Noble.

Magically Captured. Building brands for 20 years.

Jeff Noble helps everyday people celebrate life, his keen eye and witty sense of humor work magically together to record individuals of all ages and from all walks of life, doing what they do best . . . just being themselves. His striking images have helped build such brands as Ford Motor Company, Bank One, Pfizer, The Dial Corp, Ocean Spray, AT&T, The Quaker Oats Company, Arizona State University, The Arizona Republic, Harris Bank N.A., Prudential Life Insurance, Scottsdale Convention & Visitors Bureau, Westcor, The American Red Cross, United Way, Blue Cross Blue Shield, Universal Technical Institute, The American Dental Association, Philadelphia Insurance, Catholic Healthcare West, US Bank and Red Baron Pizza.

telephone: **800.777.noble 602.440.4900**
fax: **602.440.4907**
url: **www.noblestock.com**
e mail: **jeff@noblestock.com**

Greg O.

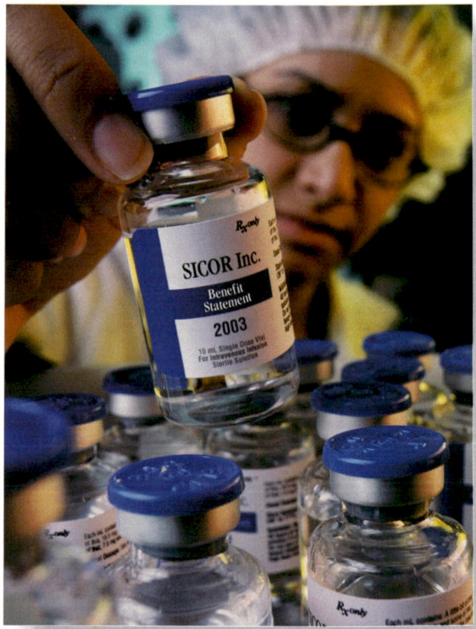

GREG O'LOUGHLIN PHOTOGRAPHY :
PHONE 949.212.1417 :
WEB www.gregO.com :

PICTUREBOY CREATIVE

847-437-3334

jonathan sprague
415.999.6616
www.jonathansprague.com

represented by REDUX 212.253.0399
www.reduxpictures.com

3def

PAULA LERNER
PHOTOGRAPHY

BOSTON • 617-489-6747

WWW.LERNERPHOTO.COM

Client: Children's Hospital Boston

Client: People Magazine

Eric Millette Photography

San Francisco

phone 415.750.9999
web www.ericmillette.com
email eric@ericmillette.com

Chris Ayers
650-961-2700
888-644-2700
chrisayers@ayersphoto.com

Brooks Sports
Business Objects
Cadence
Gilead
Habitat for Humanity
Intel Corp
KPMG Consulting
MetLife
NEC
PC World
RARE
Synopsys

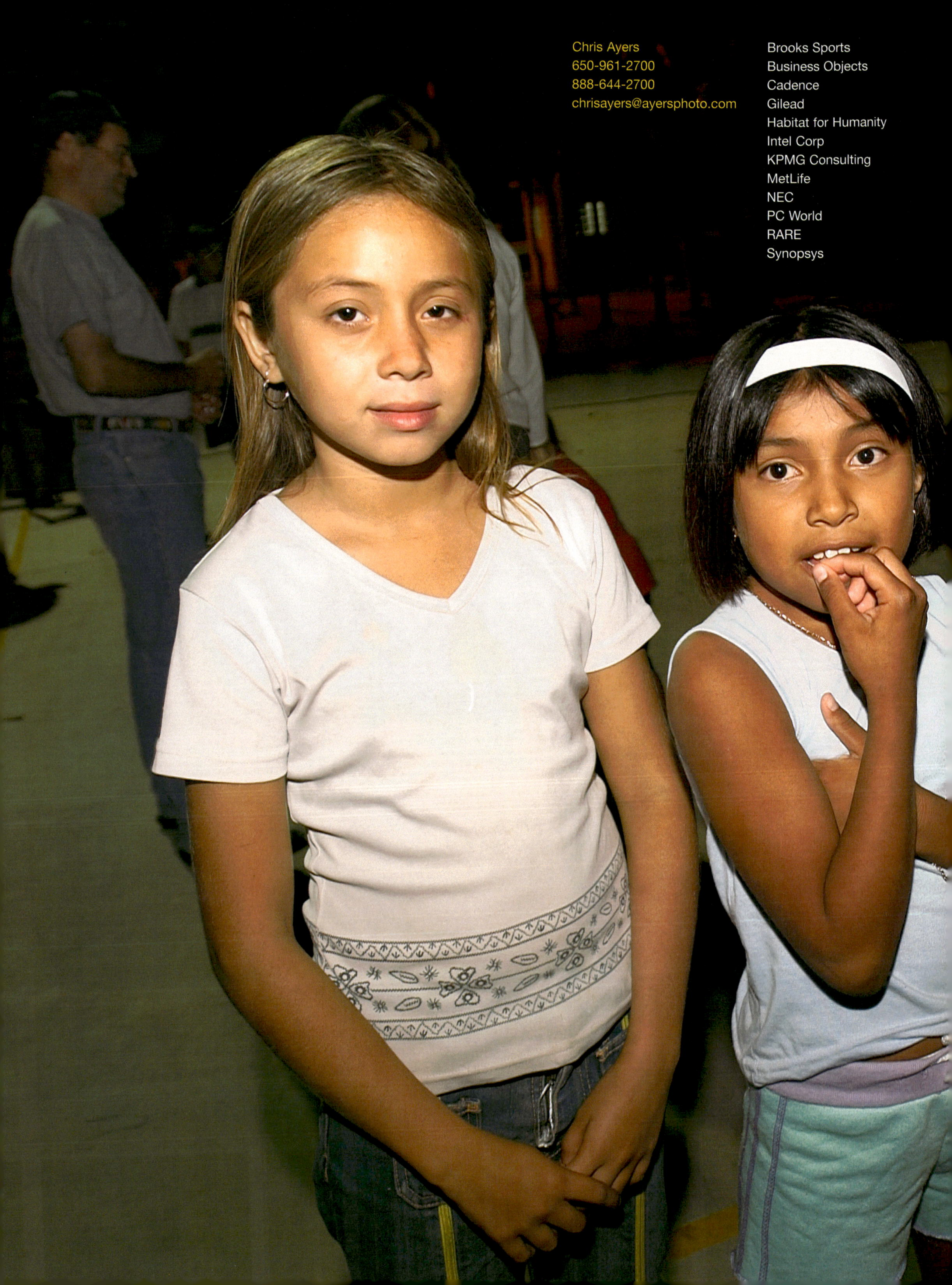

Tulum, the Yucatan Peninsula. Two days earlier I was shooting an amazing technology in Silicon Valley.

It's nice to know that inspiration can still come from anywhere.

PHOTO
UMANS
GRAPHY
marty umans
photography
represented
by hurewitz
creative
partners
212.995.0100
hurewitz.com

KEITH SKELTON PHOTOGRAPHY
213-804-1116
California Water 2003 Annual Report

KEITH SKELTON PHOTOGRAPHY
213-804-1116
Pixelworks 2003 Annual Report

Michael Paras Photography

350 7th Avenue, New York, NY 10001 • T: 212.736.7835 • paras@parasphotography.com

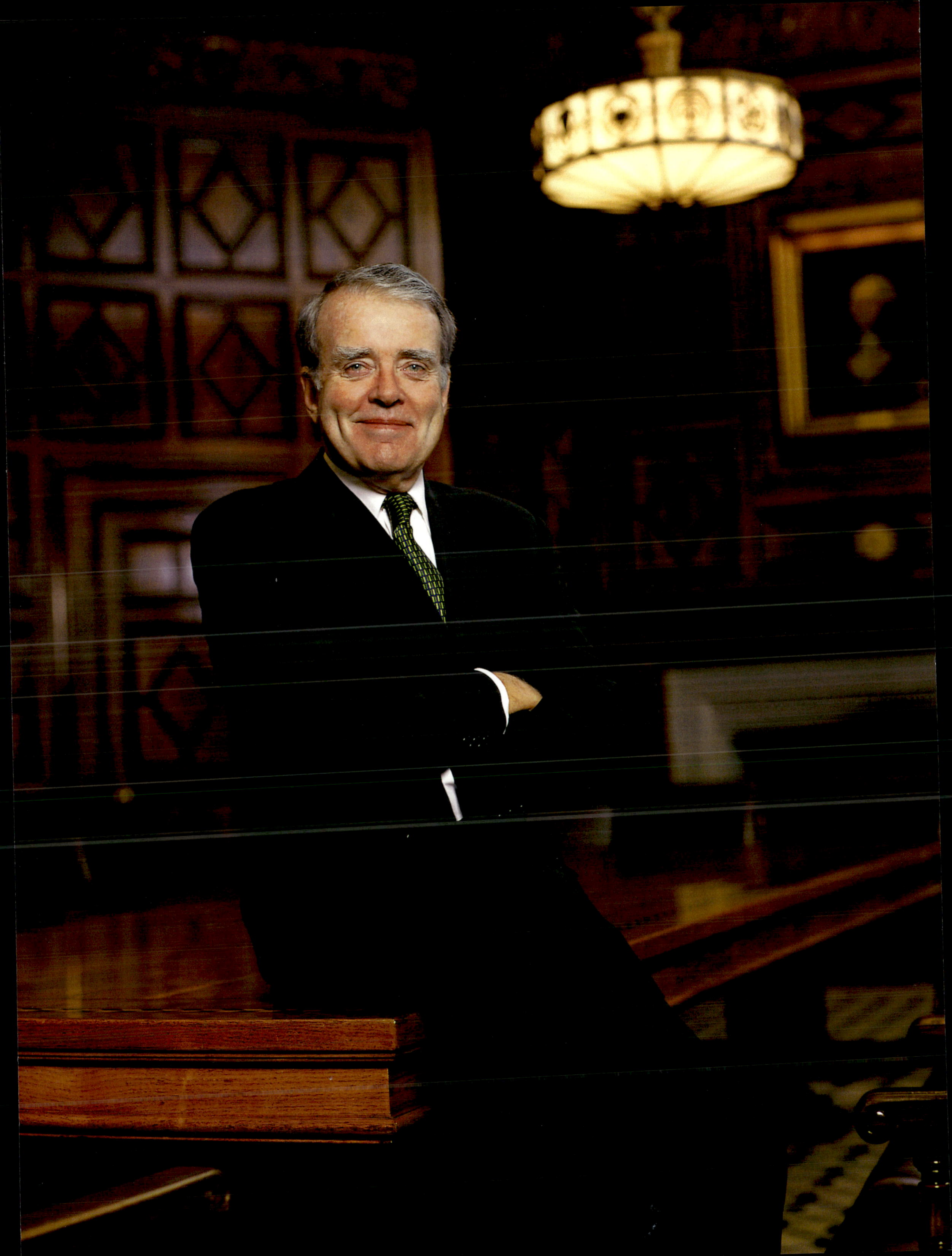

DONALD WALLER
Photography

T 212.242.0030 201.659.8606

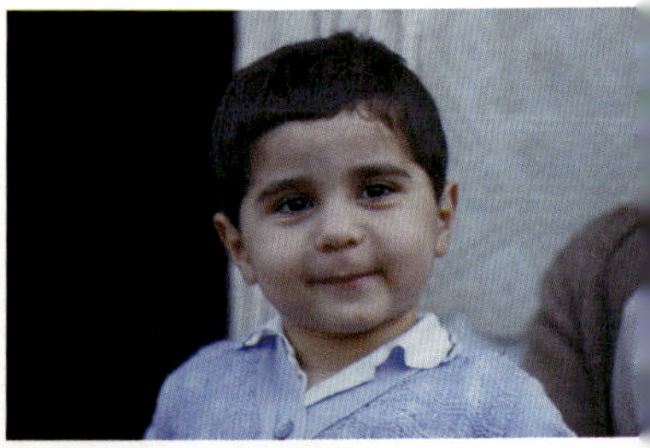

DANIEL PORTNOY
photographer

305.253.8262
www.danielportnoy.com
daniel@danielportnoy.com

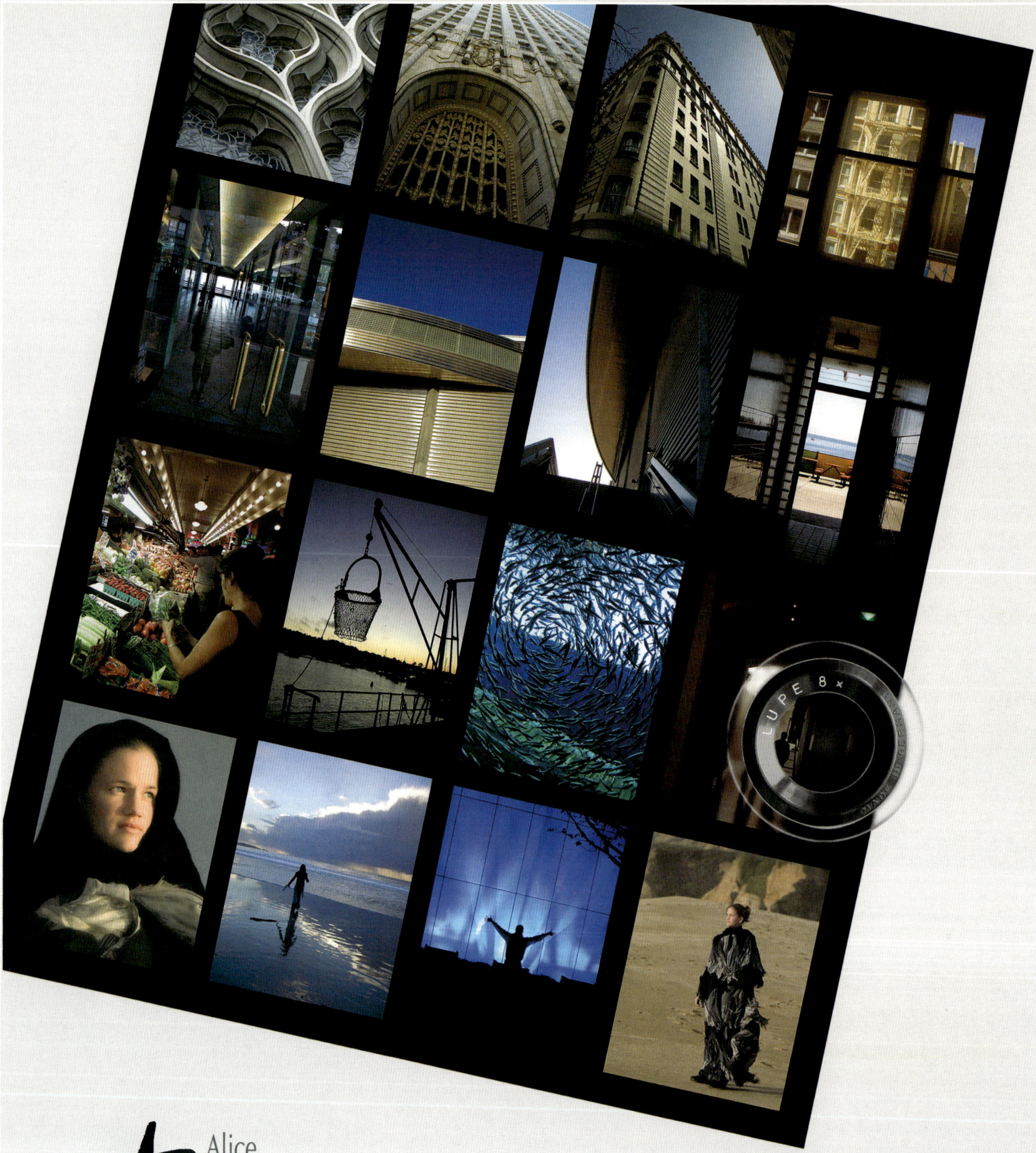
LUPE 8×

image notes:

proof positive

it takes 3 men to

change a lightbulb

in the Louvre...

maybe that's why

Mona Lisa is

always smiling!

a uthentic images...

b eautiful lighting...

c onsuming **p a s s i o n!**

alicebutterickconcepts.com
alice@butterick.org
650.917.1155

415.252.7818
roberthouser.com

robert houser
photography

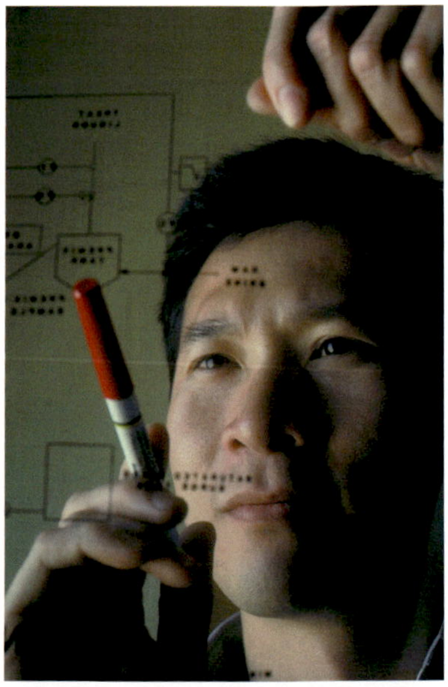

Les Wollam

tele : 214 760 7721 cell : 214 395 4732 Web : leswollamphoto.com

ALEC HUFF PHOTOGRAPHY
312.504.4885
www.alechuff.com

CLIFF KUCINE ▸ CELL 207.650.4519

LIFESTYLE

EDITORIAL
MAGAZINE

real **PEOPLE**

ANNUAL
REPORTS

real **WORK**

real **PLAY**

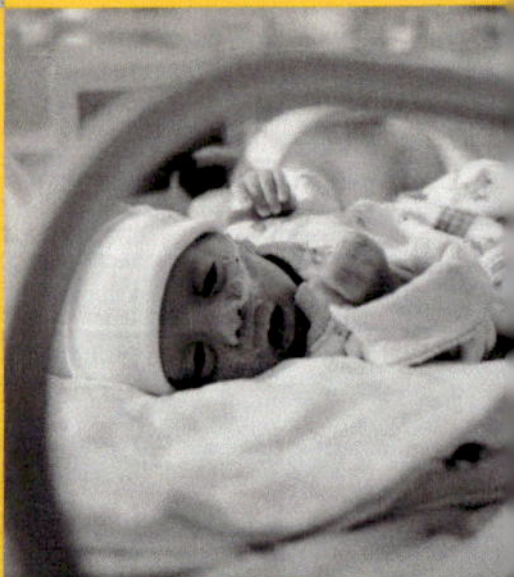

HART

MICHAEL HART PHOTOGRAPHY
WWW.HARTPHOTO.COM
713-271-8250

REPRESENTED BY
MELODY GEORGE & ASSOCIATES
713-661-6521

ROBERT NEUMANN
The American Fabric
p 616 454.1001 f 616 454.4546
a 312 ELLSWORTH GRAND RAPIDS, MI 49503
e RNEUMANN@BIGEVENTSTUDIOS.COM

Corporate and Editorial Photography

Swimmer

Computer executive

Actor Henry Thomas

Young policemen hang out in Moscow

Tram overlooking Bogota, Colombia

Natural gas platform in Lake Maricaibo, Venezuela

Energy trading in Houston

Chef and entrepreneur

Bicycle man

Salon owner and entrepreneur

BeauSoleil fiddler Michael Doucet

IT director for schools

Commuters in Tokyo subway

Energy company CEO

Software company CEO

CHIP FORELLI

industrial / inhabited / intrinsic landscape photography
assignment/licensing

photo@chipforelli.com 1-877-367-3554 www.chipforelli.com

Anessa Kemna, visually impaired 2004 Paralympic swimmer.

T 612.331.5305 W trelevenphotography.com

Xcel Energy 2003 Annual Report.

TRELEVEN PHOTOGRAPHY

Gert Boyle, CEO Columbia Sportswear

Charles Schwab

ROGER TULLY

599 FIFTH STREET
BROOKLYN, NEW YORK 11215

P: 718.768.7575
F: 718.768.7545

E-MAIL: ROGER@TULLYPHOTO.COM
WEB: WWW.TULLYPHOTO.COM

Justin Smith

PHOTOGRAPHY

K E
E P

www.artphotosite.com

People is what I do best

Djamel E. Ramoul PHOTOGRAPHER
Central Florida 352 425 8611

Florida Magazine Association Photographer of the Year 2003
Gold Charlie Award Best Color Photography 2003

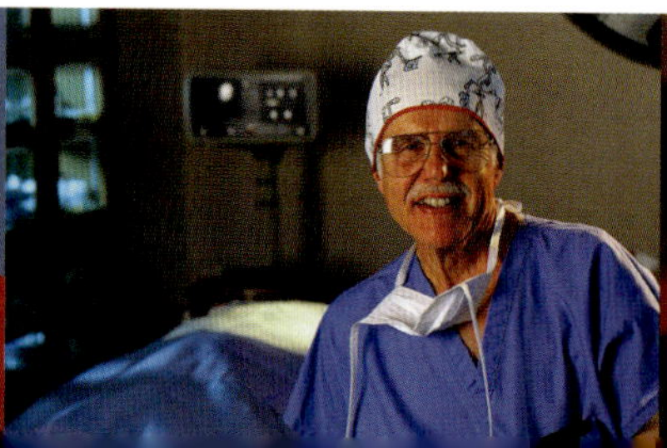

closeup

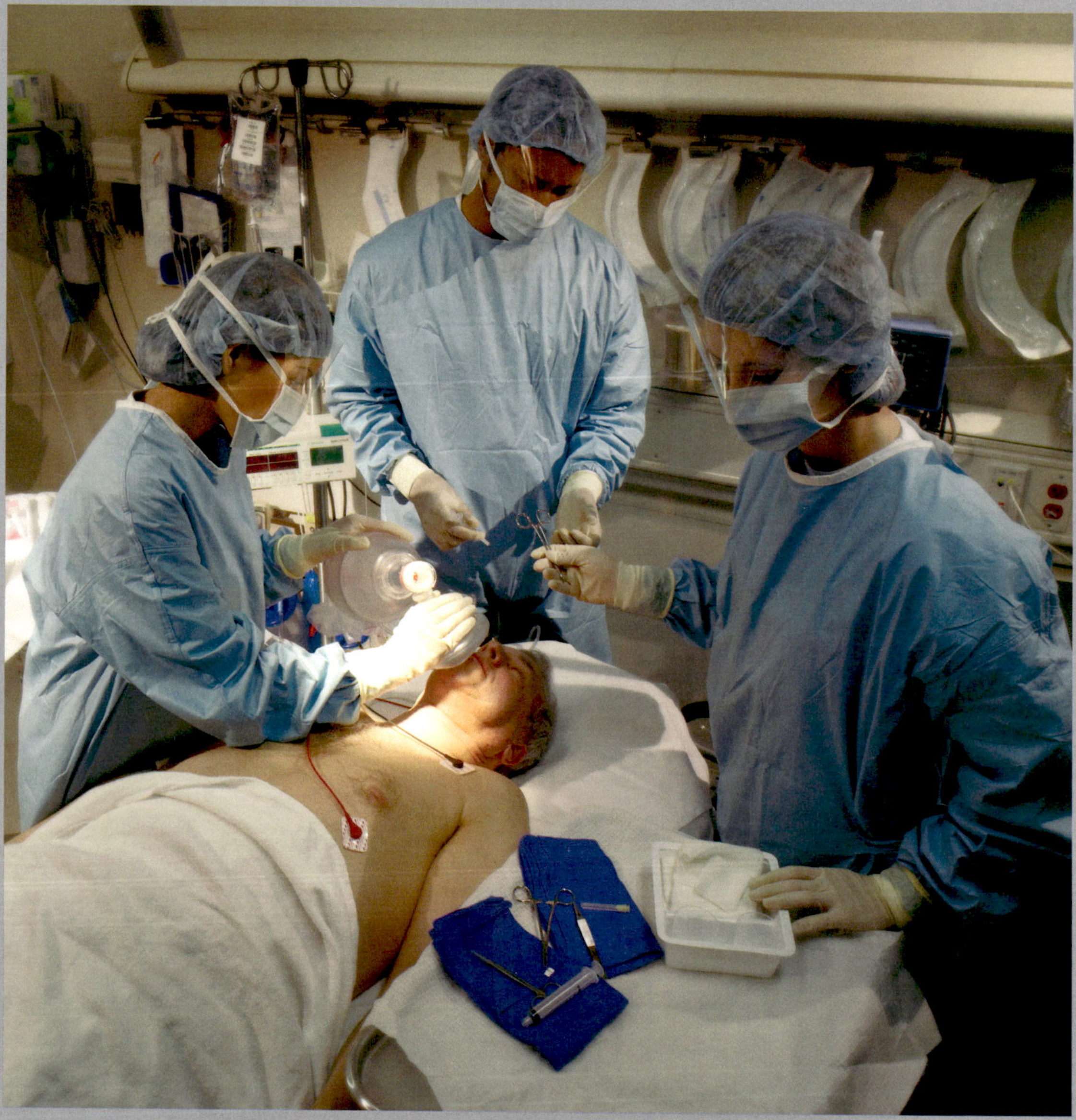

McKenzie
PHOTOGRAPHY
B. Donald McKenzie
133 W. Vermont Ave.
Southern Pines, NC. 28387
910-692-1712
Toll Free: 1-877-692-1712
Website:
www.mckenziephotography.com
E-mail:
mcfoto@pinehurst.net
McKenzie
PHOTOGRAPHY
Subject:
Corporate,
Editorial,
Industrial,
Environmental
Portraiture
Data:

DANA HURSEY PHOTOGRAPHY

www.hursey.com
TEL626/345/9996
STUDIO·LOCATION·FILM·DIGITAL

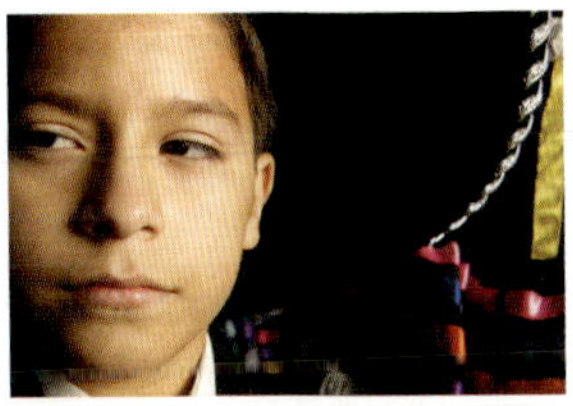

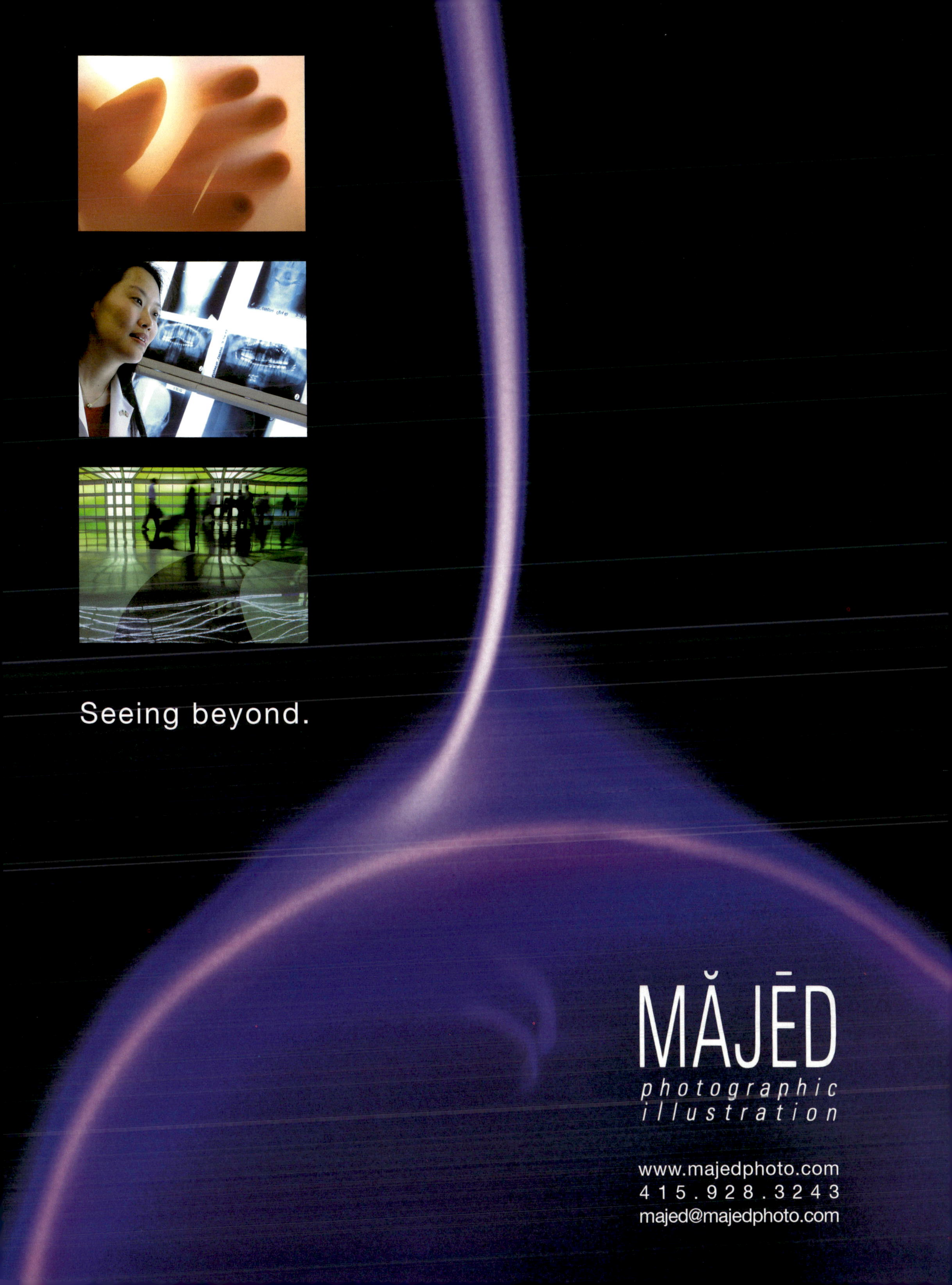
Seeing beyond.
MĂJĒD
photographic
illustration
www.majedphoto.com
415.928.3243
majed@majedphoto.com

B
END

APPLIED
MOLECULAR
EVOLUTION

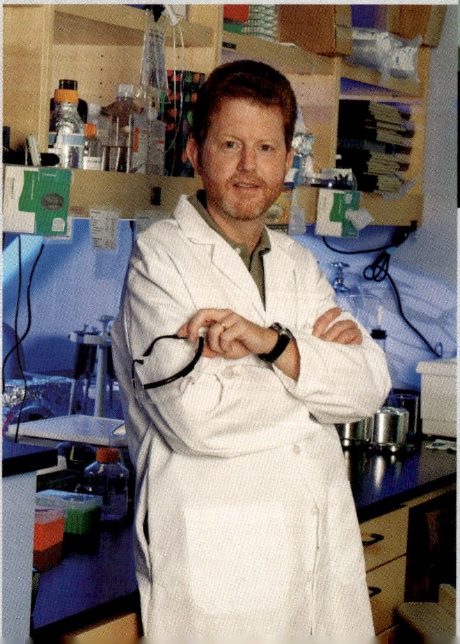

Elisa Cicinelli Photography

SAN FRANCISCO

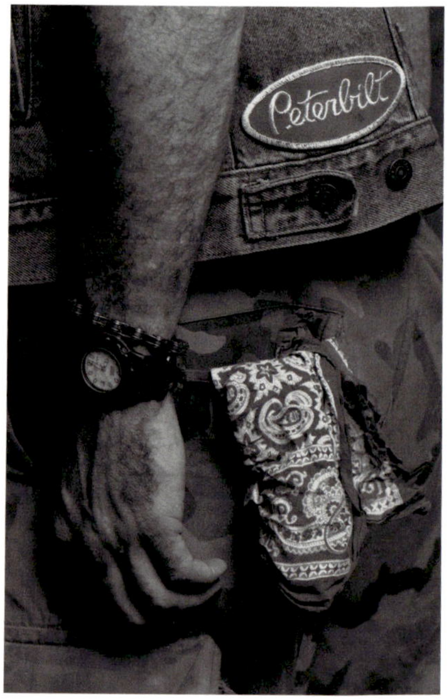

CLIENTS

Bank of America

United Way

Medtronic Minimed

phone 415.775.8944

web www.ciciphoto.com

email elisa@ciciphoto.com

BELVEDERE
VODKA
IMPORTED

Still, Inc.

photo • illustration • motion

www.johnstill.com or call 617-527-9911

clients :
3M Corporation • AdvancePCS/CareMark • AutoDesk • ARIAD • AT&T • Ball Corporation
CitiBank • Canon • IBM • Intel • MIT Medialab • S.C.Johnson Wax • Time, Inc.

➡ www.wandanow.com

MICHAEL MEISTER

FREDERIQUE BERTRAND

ELENE USDIN

MARTIN MATJE

MARIE LAFRANCE

BORIS KULIKOV

NICKY ACKLAND-SNOW

CHILDREN'S ILLUSTRATORS

STOCK ILLUSTRATIONS

REPRESENTED (by) **WANDA NOWAK**

CREATIVE ILLUSTRATORS AGENCY

PHONE 212·535·0438 FAX 212·535·1624

WALL
N 34.450 ▼ 0.110 AME 26.850 ▲ 0.240 AP 12.900 ▼ 0.050 APH 31.760
609 823 2420
mmorgenstern.com
macworld new yorker newsweek new york times polygram random house sony wall street journal

www.jamesyang.com

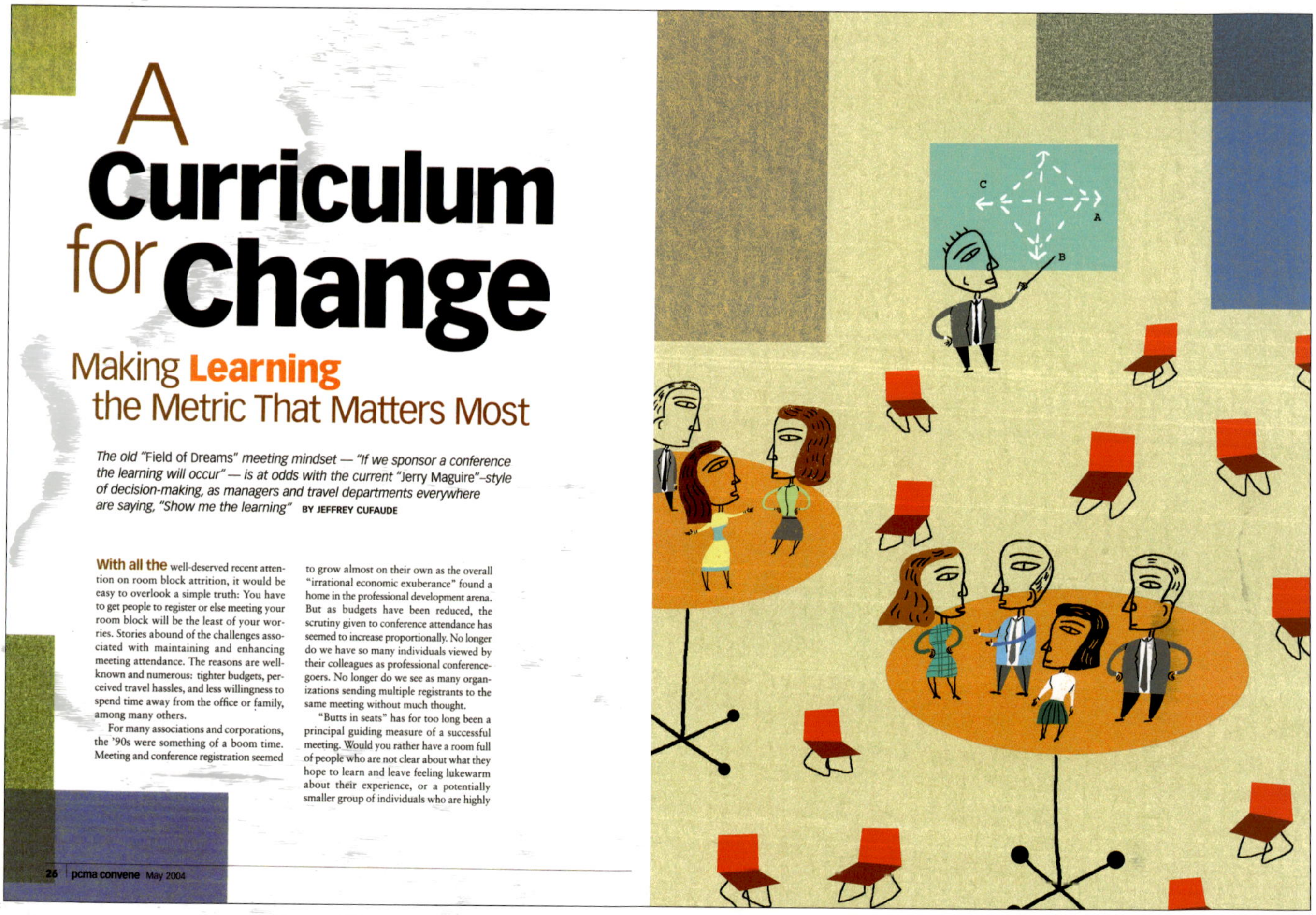

A Curriculum for Change

Making Learning the Metric That Matters Most

The old "Field of Dreams" meeting mindset — "If we sponsor a conference the learning will occur" — is at odds with the current "Jerry Maguire"–style of decision-making, as managers and travel departments everywhere are saying, "Show me the learning" BY JEFFREY CUFAUDE

With all the well-deserved recent attention on room block attrition, it would be easy to overlook a simple truth: You have to get people to register or else meeting your room block will be the least of your worries. Stories abound of the challenges associated with maintaining and enhancing meeting attendance. The reasons are well-known and numerous: tighter budgets, perceived travel hassles, and less willingness to spend time away from the office or family, among many others.

For many associations and corporations, the '90s were something of a boom time. Meeting and conference registration seemed to grow almost on their own as the overall "irrational economic exuberance" found a home in the professional development arena. But as budgets have been reduced, the scrutiny given to conference attendance has seemed to increase proportionally. No longer do we have so many individuals viewed by their colleagues as professional conference-goers. No longer do we see as many organizations sending multiple registrants to the same meeting without much thought.

"Butts in seats" has for too long been a principal guiding measure of a successful meeting. Would you rather have a room full of people who are not clear about what they hope to learn and leave feeling lukewarm about their experience, or a potentially smaller group of individuals who are highly

26 | pcma convene May 2004

JAMES YANG is proudly Represented by DAVID GOLDMAN AGENCY
41 Union Square West, Suite 918, New York, NY 10003
Ph: 212-807-6627 Fax: 212-463-8175 www.davidgoldmanagency.com

DININNO

STEVE DININNO/www.stevedininno.com is proudly Represented by DAVID GOLDMAN AGENCY
41 Union Square West, Suite 918, New York, NY 10003
Ph: 212-807-6627 Fax: 212-463-8175 www.davidgoldmanagency.com

MICHELLE BARNES

Discover Magazine

St Martin s Press

The New York Times Magazine

Port of Seattle Annual Report

MICHELLE BARNES/www.michellebarnes.com is proudly Represented by DAVID GOLDMAN AGENCY
41 Union Square West, Suite 918, New York, NY 10003
Ph: 212-807-6627 Fax: 212-463-8175 www.davidgoldmanagency.com

NORM BENDELL/www.bendellstudio.com is proudly Represented by DAVID GOLDMAN AGENCY
41 Union Square West, Suite 918, New York, NY 10003
Ph: 212-807-6627 Fax: 212-463-8175 www.davidgoldmanagency.com

MATTHEW STRAUSS

The dented lifestyle • INTERVIEW: A taste of Alsace
The Boston Globe Magazine
FREE MICKEY!
A new copyright law keeps thousands of books, movies, and songs in private hands. Can a New Hampshire bibliophile's crusade reclaim them for the public? *By Daren Fonda*

MATTHEW STRAUSS/www.mstrauss.com is proudly Represented by DAVID GOLDMAN AGENCY
41 Union Square West, Suite 918, New York, NY 10003
Ph: 212-807-6627 Fax: 212-463-8175 www.davidgoldmanagency.com

WESSLER 3-D ILLUSTRATION

[This is NOT photography.]

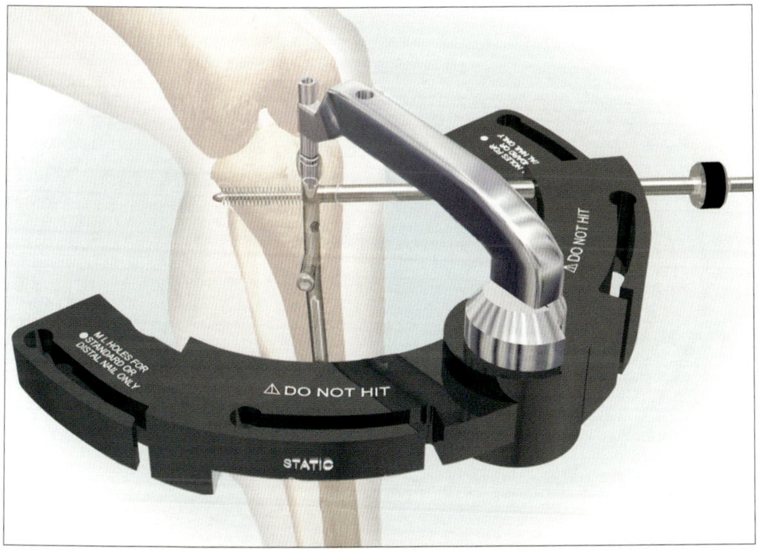

RICK WESSLER/www.wessler3d.com is proudly Represented by DAVID GOLDMAN AGENCY
41 Union Square West, Suite 918, New York, NY 10003
Ph: 212-807-6627 Fax: 212-463-8175 www.davidgoldmanagency.com

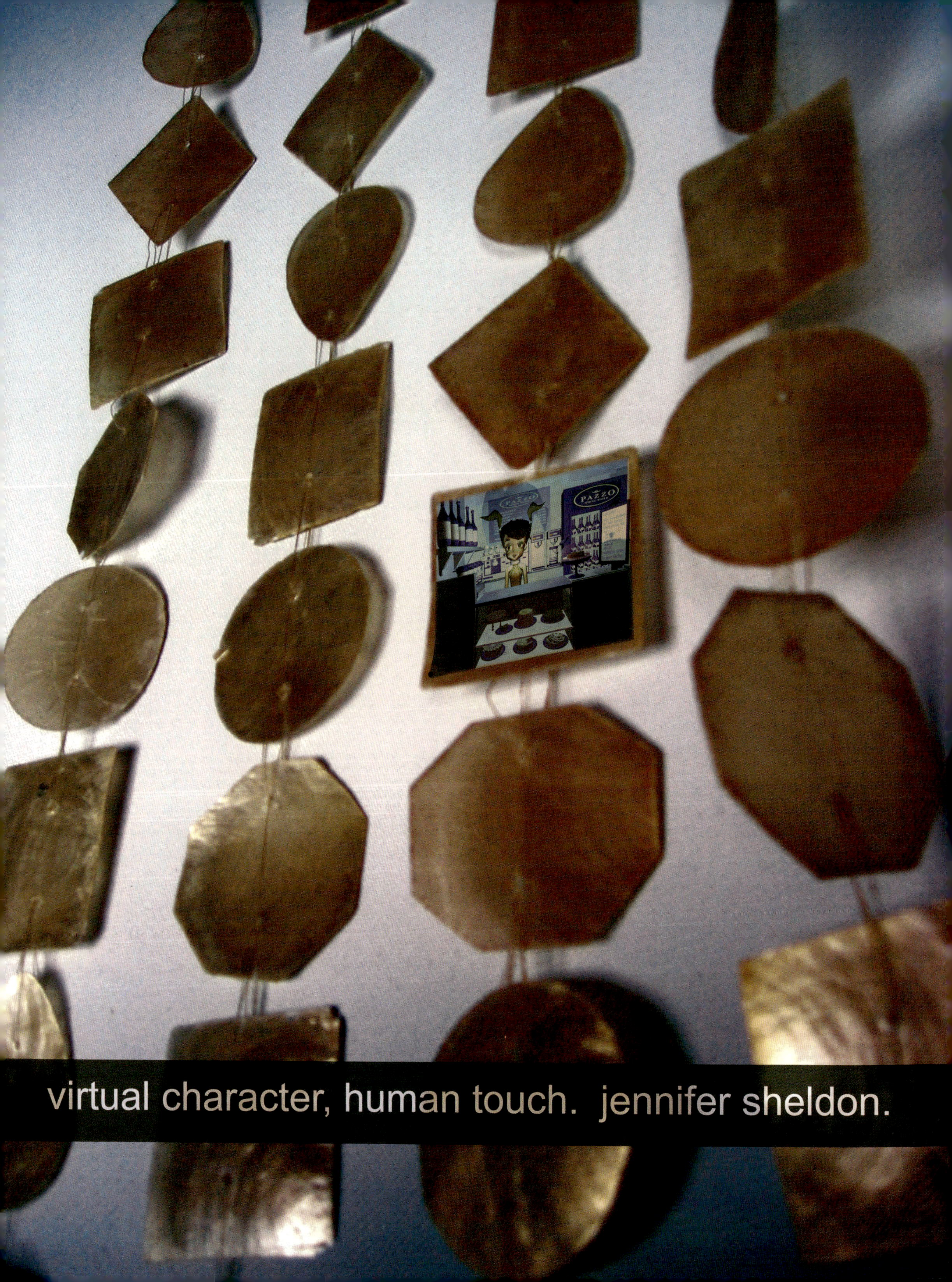

virtual character, human touch. jennifer sheldon.

GREG • NEWBOLD

KLEENEX • SONY PICTURES • HEINZ FOODS • SMUCKER'S • CADILLAC • HEWLETT PACKARD
SIMON & SCHUSTER • RANDOM HOUSE • HARPER COLLINS • BANTAM / DOUBLEDAY / DELL

801.274.2407 • WWW.GREGNEWBOLD.COM

Andy Zito

Superb concept images for all categories and for all media

135 South La Brea Ave.
Los Angeles, CA 90036
TEL 323-931-1182
FAX 323-931-3091
Email: andyzito@hotmail.com
www.andyzito.com

Chicago:
Koralik Associates
TEL 815-777-0420
FAX 815-777-0488
Email: korkeel@netexpress.net
www.koralikassoc.com

New York:
American Artists
TEL 212-682-2462
FAX 212-582-0090
Email: mike@aareps.com
www.amerartists.com

pepper tharp

tel 612. 978. 8383

e peppert@visi.com

w peppertharp.com

pepper tharp

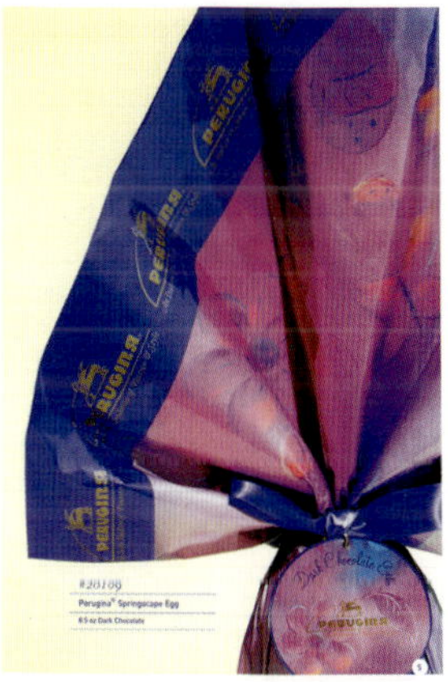

American Airlines
American West
American Express
Baci
Boston Children's Hospital
Briggs & Stratton
Nestle
Perugina
Target
Talbot's
Tyndale
St. Martin's Press
Gallo
Harlequin
Lord & Taylor
Marshall Field's
Meredith
MSP Publications

Aaron Charles Rhymes
www.ACillustrations.com tel: 510 734 9089

LLOYD MILLER

Illustration & Graphic Design

www.millerillustration.com

212.505.5767

DIRECT MAIL

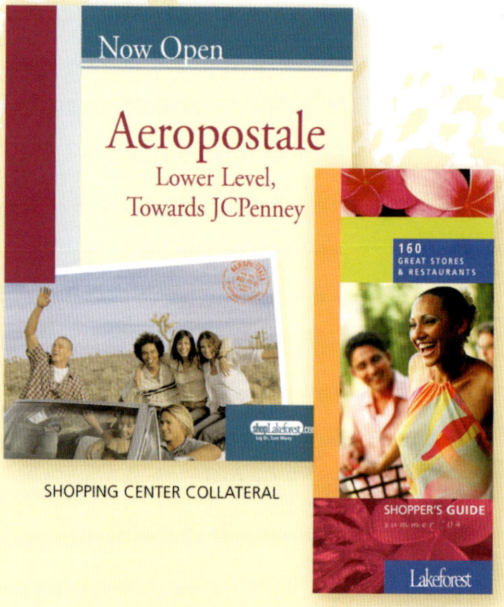

SHOPPING CENTER COLLATERAL

NIST TCal

LOGOS

Linda Sherman Design

FINE ART

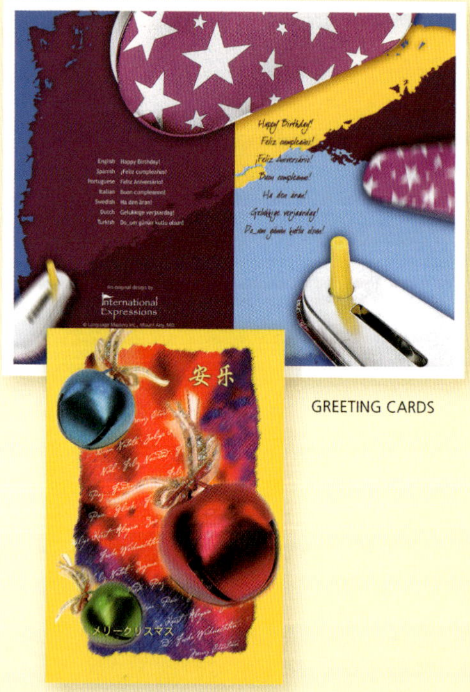

GREETING CARDS

PRODUCT CATALOGS

STRAYER EDUCATION

DALLAS
PREVENTIVE FAMILY THERAPY

Linda Sherman Design 301.590.0604 ★ FAX: 301.590.0605 ★ WWW.LSHERMANDESIGN.COM

SMALL STUDIO, BIG RESULTS

PANTONE® 614 U
PANTONE® 125 U
PANTONE® 140 U
PANTONE® 175 U
PANTONE® 1545 U
PANTONE® 4525 U
PANTONE® 614 U
PANTONE® 4525 U
PANTONE® 614 U
PANTONE® 125 U
PANTONE® 4525 U
WHITE U
PANTONE® 175 U
WHITE U
PANTONE® 614 U
PANTONE® 4525 U
PANTONE® 614 U

Need a little boost?
cap.
out of order
103 pt
93 pt
3 pt
PANTONE®
641 U
pms 641
Sabon Roman?

Ar

AA winners

As makers of the finest
uncoated printing papers
in the industry, we support
your quest for excellence.
Rock on.
Need a climbing partner?
Monadnock Paper Mills, Inc.
Bennington, New Hampshire 03442
For samples, product information and technical assistance,
please call 877.877.2098 or visit www.mpm.com.
Monadnock

m·real
WE PLAY FOR

Centura
Productolith
Fortune
Orion

We have more than goofy smiles, firm handshakes and superb printing. We have cable.
We love to see you, greet you and entertain you. But honestly, our passion is in our printing. Each one of us lives to make you look good. Our numerous awards this past 2003 annual report season could not have been earned any other way. For more information, give us a call at 323.261.7171 or visit www.colorgraphics.com.
Los Angeles
San Francisco
Seattle
Orange County
ColorGraphics
Making you look good

The Incomparable Source Books
For Creative Talent

The Black Book Photography

The Black Book Illustration

Creative Industry Directory

Ar

100

19

Ar winners

Ar

THE AR 100

Best of Show

{MOST INNOVATIVE CONCEPT}
{JUDGES AWARD}
{BEST COVER DESIGN}
{BEST PHOTOGRAPHED}

{BEST USE OF PAPER}
{BEST PRINTED}
{BEST USE OF TYPOGRAPHY}
{BEST ILLUSTRATED}

1

Zumtobel AG

FIRM_	sagmeister inc.
ART DIRECTOR_	stefan sagmeister
DESIGNER_	matthias ernstberger
PHOTOGRAPHER_	bela borsodi
COPYWRITER_	otto riewoldt
PRINTERS_	veronaprint; cover: zumtobel staff, reiss international

{ A unique, one-of-a-kind annual report. I don't think this could ever be done in the united states. such a simple, high-concept book. An actual object, with its vac-u-formed front and back covers. An art piece that leaves me with a glowing impression of the company.}

- Kent Hunter

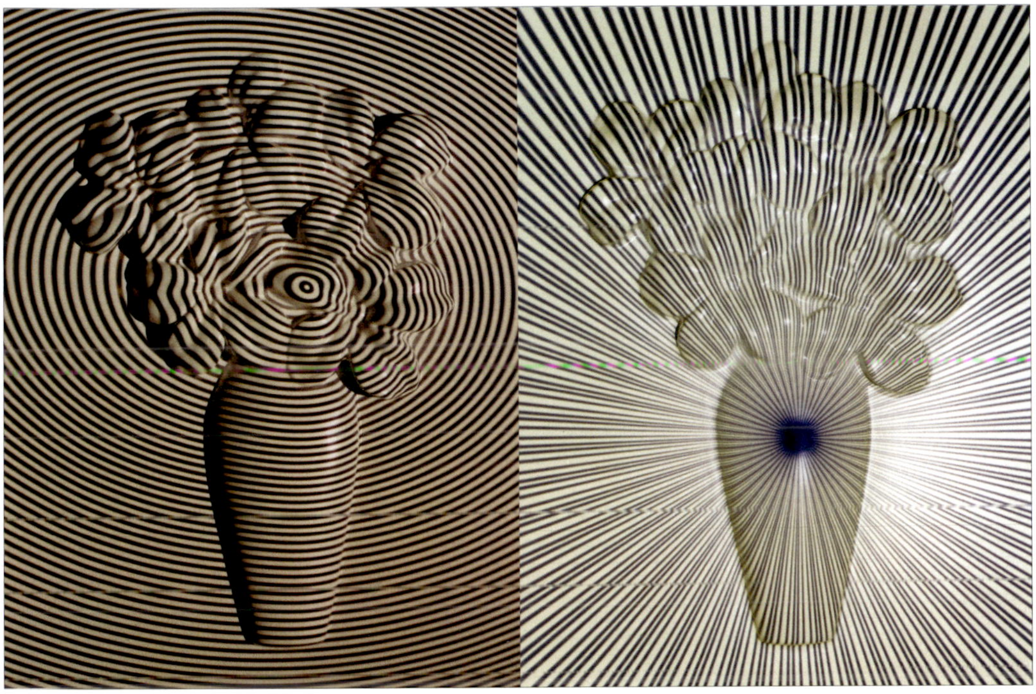

TEXT PAPER	150G. Luxosatin
PAGES	108
QUANTITY	5,000

MFI

FIRM_	SAS
ART DIRECTORS_	Andy Spencer, Gilmar Wendt, David Stocks
DESIGNERS_	Andy Spencer, Manja Hellpap
PHOTOGRAPHER_	Matt Stuart
COPYWRITER_	Martin Peacock
PRINTER_	Fulmar Colour Printing

{ The simple, unexpected and humorous approach to this annual report sets it apart from all others. Visuals of a normal family living and doing everyday things in a public store environment shows off both the store and the livability of all the furniture and appliances MFI sells. This was a brilliant idea and could be the basis for a new reality show!}

- David Stoyan Wooters

COVER PAPER	300GSM GF Smith Zen Pure
TEXT PAPER	150GSM GF Smith Zen Pure
COLORS	5
PAGES	77
QUANTITY	25,000

WD40

FIRM_	Turner & Associates
ART DIRECTORS_	Laurie Carrigan, Steve Turner
DESIGNER_	Laura Milton
PHOTOGRAPHER_	Jock McDonald
COPYWRITER_	Brad Londy
PRINTER_	Anderson Lithograph

{ I loved this book. 50 fun facts about WD-40. A true celebration of a product and the cult(ure) around it. How many companies have a fan club? outstanding copywriting and fun, skim-able format. Loved the "50 Impostors" page (Nuts off, Really Good S--T) and the "50 uses in 50 states" (Nevada-Lubricates drive system of dollar bill changers). Inventive, amusing and entertaining. Three things lacking in most annual reports. I'm buying the stock. }

- Kent Hunter

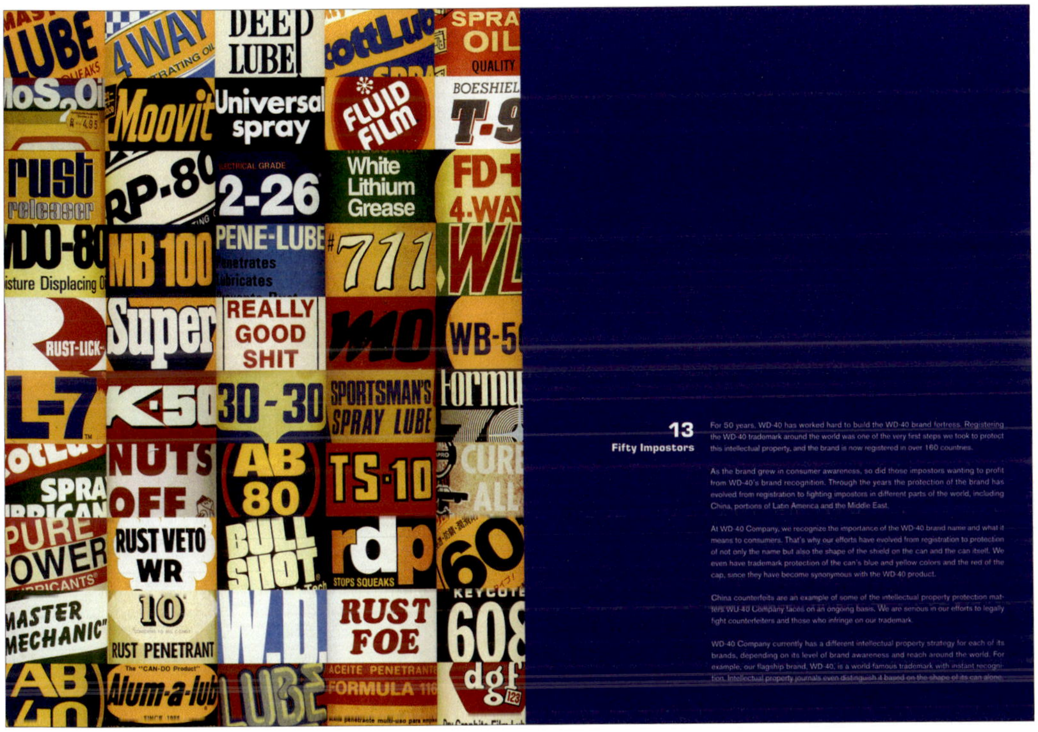

COVER PAPER	100lb. New Leaf Pax
TEXT PAPER	80lb. New Leaf Pax
COLORS	6
PAGES	44
QUANTITY	22,000

SPCA of Texas

FIRM_	RBMM
ART DIRECTORS_	Steve Gibbs, Dick Mitchell, Brian Boyd
DESIGNER_	Brian Owens
ILLUSTRATOR	David Vaught
PHOTOGRAPHERS_	Peter Kao (cover), Joe Grisham, Chris Whalen, Mark Bumgarner, John Wong, Robie Capps, Tadd Myers, Heather Ezell
COPYWRITERS_	David Culp, Kathy Edwards
PRINTER_	Williamson Printing Corporation

{ A great cover has to be eye-catching and this one is. A clever use of dog leashes laid side by side creates a colorful and intriguing cover that begs to be picked up and opened. }

- David Stoyan Wooters

{ As a native Texan, I loved this cover. I especially liked that they didn't choose the easy out of an adorable kitten or puppy pic. The colorful collars and Texas shaped dog tag got my attention right away. }

- Kent Hunter

COVER PAPER	80lb. Cougar Smooth Cover
TEXT PAPERS	65lb. Cougar Smooth Cover, 60lb Lynx Smooth Book
COLORS	4
PAGES	28
QUANTITY	30,000

Alberta Ballet

FIRM_ nu
ART DIRECTOR_ Monique Gamache
PHOTOGRAPHER_ Clay Stang
COPYWRITER_ Daniel Gibbons
PRINTER_ Sundog Printing

{ The lone ballerina pictured in an industrial garage or a deserted street are subjects in a tale not quite belonging to one another. Through the photographer's eyes, we are inspired to see beauty, elegance and poetry. }

-Anna Tan

COVER PAPER	80lb. cougar opaque Text
COLORS	5
PAGES	24
QUANTITY	2,000

Intrawest Corporation

FIRM_ SamataMason
ART DIRECTORS_ Dave Mason, Pamela Lee
DESIGNERS_ Pamela Lee, Keith Leinweber
PHOTOGRAPHERS_ Various
ILLUSTRATOR_ Keith Leinweber
PRINTER_ Blanchette Press

{ A perfect tie in to a company that develops mountain and golf resorts, these simple and fun line art illustrations compel the viewer to take a closer look at what could otherwise be several boring charts and graphs. }

- David Stoyan Wooters

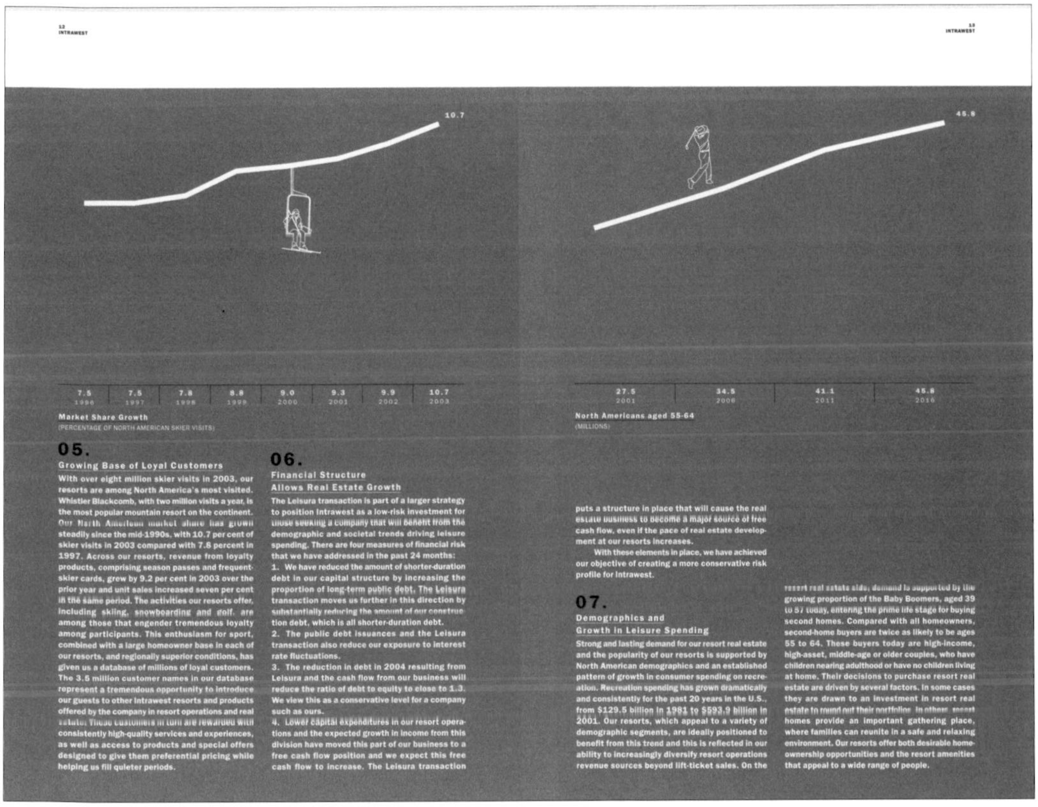

INTRAWEST

7.5	7.5	7.8	8.8	9.0	9.3	9.9	10.7
1996	1997	1998	1999	2000	2001	2002	2003

Market Share Growth
(PERCENTAGE OF NORTH AMERICAN SKIER VISITS)

05.

Growing Base of Loyal Customers

With over eight million skier visits in 2003, our resorts are among North America's most visited. Whistler Blackcomb, with two million visits a year, is the most popular mountain resort on the continent. Our North American market share has grown steadily since the mid-1990s, with 10.7 per cent of skier visits in 2003 compared with 7.8 percent in 1997. Across our resorts, revenue from loyalty products, comprising season passes and frequent-skier cards, grew by 9.2 per cent in 2003 over the prior year and unit sales increased seven per cent in the same period. The activities our resorts offer, including skiing, snowboarding and golf, are among those that engender tremendous loyalty among participants. This enthusiasm for sport, combined with a large homeowner base in each of our resorts, and regionally superior conditions, has given us a database of millions of loyal customers. The 3.5 million customer names in our database represent a tremendous opportunity to introduce our guests to other Intrawest resorts and products offered by the company in resort operations and real estate. These customers in turn are rewarded with consistently high-quality services and experiences, as well as access to products and special offers designed to give them preferential pricing while helping us fill quieter periods.

06.

Financial Structure Allows Real Estate Growth

The Leisura transaction is part of a larger strategy to position Intrawest as a low-risk investment for those seeking a company that will benefit from the demographic and societal trends driving leisure spending. There are four measures of financial risk that we have addressed in the past 24 months:

1. We have reduced the amount of shorter-duration debt in our capital structure by increasing the proportion of long-term public debt. The Leisura transaction moves us further in this direction by substantially reducing the amount of our construction debt, which is all shorter-duration debt.
2. The public debt issuances and the Leisura transaction also reduce our exposure to interest rate fluctuations.
3. The reduction in debt in 2004 resulting from Leisura and the cash flow from our business will reduce the ratio of debt to equity to close to 1.3. We view this as a conservative level for a company such as ours.
4. Lower capital expenditures in our resort operations and the expected growth in income from this division have moved this part of our business to a free cash flow position and we expect this free cash flow to increase. The Leisura transaction puts a structure in place that will cause the real estate business to become a major source of free cash flow, even if the pace of real estate development at our resorts increases.

With these elements in place, we have achieved our objective of creating a more conservative risk profile for Intrawest.

INTRAWEST

27.5	34.5	41.1	45.9
2001	2006	2011	2016

North Americans aged 55-64
(MILLIONS)

07.

Demographics and Growth in Leisure Spending

Strong and lasting demand for our resort real estate and the popularity of our resorts is supported by North American demographics and an established pattern of growth in consumer spending on recreation. Recreation spending has grown dramatically and consistently for the past 20 years in the U.S., from $129.5 billion in 1981 to $593.9 billion in 2001. Our resorts, which appeal to a variety of demographic segments, are ideally positioned to benefit from this trend and this is reflected in our ability to increasingly diversify resort operations revenue sources beyond lift-ticket sales. On the resort real estate side, demand is supported by the growing proportion of the Baby Boomers, aged 39 to 57 today, entering the prime life stage for buying second homes. Compared with all homeowners, second-home buyers are twice as likely to be ages 55 to 64. These buyers today are high-income, high-asset, middle-age or older couples, who have children nearing adulthood or have no children living at home. Their decisions to purchase resort real estate are driven by several factors. In some cases they are drawn to an investment in resort real estate to round out their portfolios. In others, resort homes provide an important gathering place, where families can reunite in a safe and relaxing environment. Our resorts offer both desirable home-ownership opportunities and the resort amenities that appeal to a wide range of people.

COVER PAPER	80lb. Fraser Papers Pegasus Vellum Cover
TEXT PAPERS	70lb. Fraser Papers Pegasus Vellum Text, 80lb. Domtar Luna Silk Text
COLORS	7
PAGES	64
QUANTITY	25,000

Marguerite Casey Foundation

FIRM_	Methodologie
ART DIRECTOR_	Anne Traver
DESIGNER_	Minh Nguyen
PHOTOGRAPHERS_	Mary Jo McConahay, Young Lee, Kathleen King
COPYWRITERS_	Mary Jo McConahay, David Brotherton
PRINTER_	Colorgraphics

{ How do we speak? How do we communicate? The typography in this AR is a visual presentation of the human voice. It speaks gently when it has to. It shouts loudly and makes a point. All right...I hear what you're saying. }

- Anna Tan

{ This book is beautiful without being self-indulgent. The typography weaves a rich tapestry throughout, reflecting the complex and differing voices of its subject matter. }

- Dean Martin

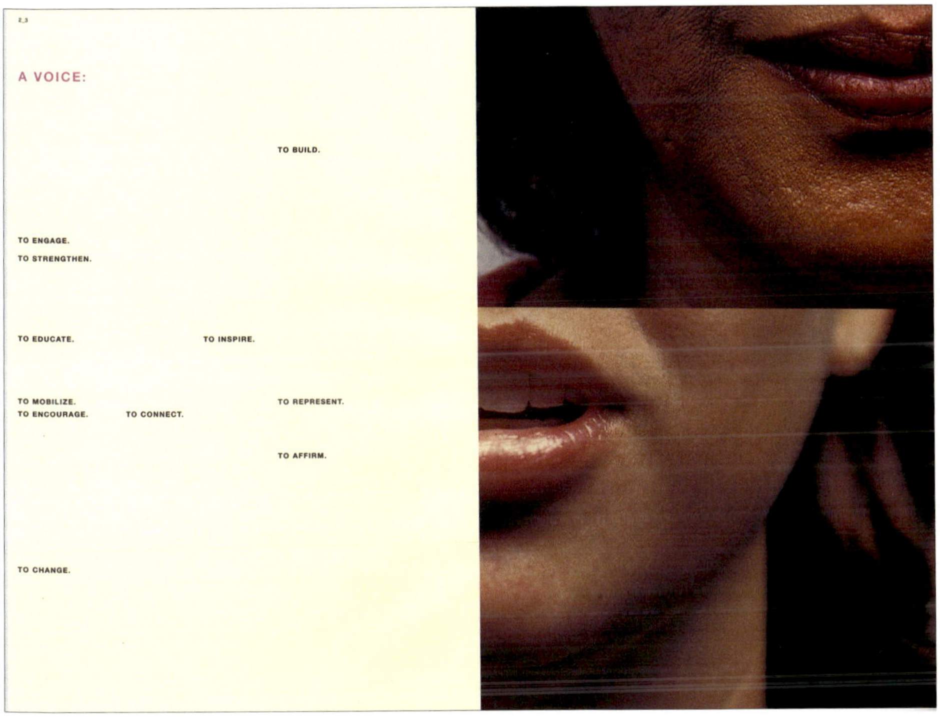

COVER PAPERS	100lb. Finch Fine Vanilla Cover; poster cover wrap on Foster Brights Gold
TEXT PAPER	100lb. Finch Fine Vanilla Text
COLORS	6
PAGES	32
QUANTITY	3,000

Quiksilver

FIRM_ Stoyan Design
ART DIRECTORS_ David Stoyan Wooters, Chi Hang
DESIGNER_ Chi Hang
PHOTOGRAPHERS_ various
PRINTER_ Colorgraphics

{ The color and quality of printing plays a crucial role in conveying the message: "Quiksilver. No words needed." The structure of the first half of the report involves a succession of vivid photographs which display surf culture at its finest. Colors were used with such intensity and impact that it truly presents Quiksilver in a vibrant light. }

- Anna Tan

COVER PAPER	60lb. Weyerhaeuser Cougar Text
TEXT PAPER	60lb. Weyerhaeuser Cougar Text
COLORS	8
PAGES	130
QUANTITY	15,000

SITEL Corporation

FIRM_	David Day + Associates
ART DIRECTOR_	David Day
DESIGNER_	Jill Rizzo
PHOTOGRAPHER_	Malone and Company
ILLUSTRATOR_	Jill Rizzo
COPYWRITER_	Nena Brabec
PRINTER_	Omaha Print

{ The use of vellum in this piece literally provides an additional layer of meaning to the narrative - in this case, a material choice of materials. }

- Dean Martin

COVER PAPER	100lb. Anthem Matte Cover
TEXT PAPER	100lb. Anthem Matte Text
COLORS	6
PAGES	56
QUANTITY	20,000

Top

10 Designed

AW_ {AWARD WINNER}
AW_ {AWARD WINNER}
AW_ {AWARD WINNER}
AW_ {AWARD WINNER}
AW_ {AWARD WINNER}

COVER PAPER 80lb. Mohawk options 100% PC white
TEXT PAPER 80lb. Mohawk options 100% PC white
COLORS 8
PAGES 120
QUANTITY 126,000

BP

FIRM_ VSA Partners
ART DIRECTORS_ Dana Arnett, Jamie Koval
DESIGNERS_ Dan Knuckey, Brock Conrad
PHOTOGRAPHERS_ Various
COPYWRITER_ Andy Blankenburg
PRINTERS_ Sandy Alexander, St. Ives Burrups

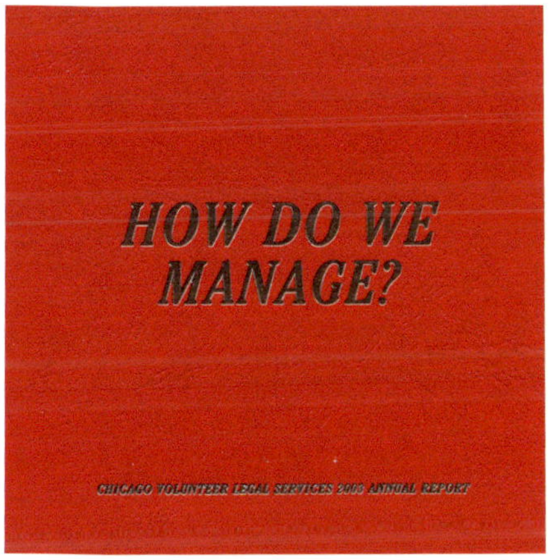

COLORS	2
PAGES	96
QUANTITY	5,000

Chicago Volunteer Legal Services

FIRM_	Lowercase, Inc.
ART DIRECTOR_	Tim Bruce
DESIGNER_	Tim Bruce
PHOTOGRAPHER_	Tony Armour
PRINTER_	Blanchette Press

Children's Home & Aid Society of Illinois 2003 Annual Report

COVER PAPER	100lb. sappi Mccoy matte cover
TEXT PAPER	80lb. sappi Mccoy matte text
COLORS	5
PAGES	44
QUANTITY	4,000

"The Rice Center was a big help. I want to do something for CHASI. If I had a lot of money, I'd give it to the Rice Center. There are a lot of children there that need help...It's a good place for children that want to work out their problems."
- Bryan

"I want to thank the staff at the Rice Center. We couldn't have survived without them. They gave me hope...We all changed for the better."
- Tiwana

Children's Home and Aid Society

FIRM_	samatamason
ART DIRECTOR_	Greg samata
DESIGNER_	Beth May
PHOTOGRAPHERS_	chris Kirzeder, stock
COPYWRITER_	Betty Brisk
PRINTER_	Blanchette press

COVER PAPER	80lb. Fox River Confetti
TEXT PAPER	65lb. Mohawk Options
COLORS	5
PAGES	51
QUANTITY	11,000

Cost Plus World Market

FIRM_	Turner & Associates
ART DIRECTOR_	Steve Turner
DESIGNER_	Laura Milton
PHOTOGRAPHERS_	Angie Wyant, Jock McDonald
COPYWRITER_	Terry London
PRINTER_	Watermark Press

COVER PAPER	.088 board casebound black pearl linen
TEXT PAPER	100lb. sappi mccoy matte text, 80lb. mohawk warm white vellum text
COLORS	8
PAGES	86
QUANTITY	10,000

Courier Corporation

FIRM_	weymouth design
ART DIRECTOR_	robert krivicich
DESIGNER_	aaron haesaert
PHOTOGRAPHER_	michael weymouth
COPYWRITER_	john temple
PRINTER_	quebecor world acme

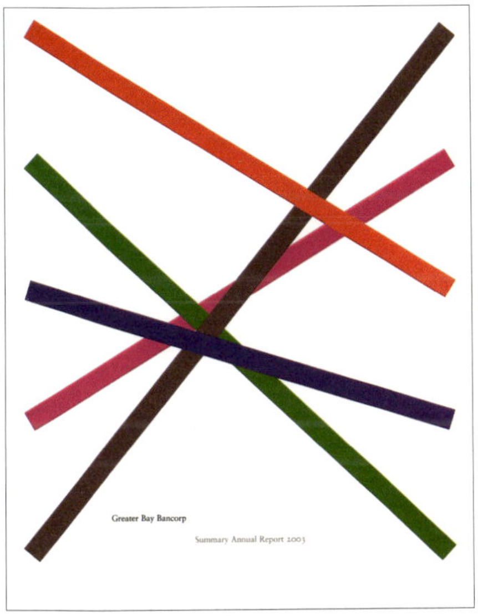

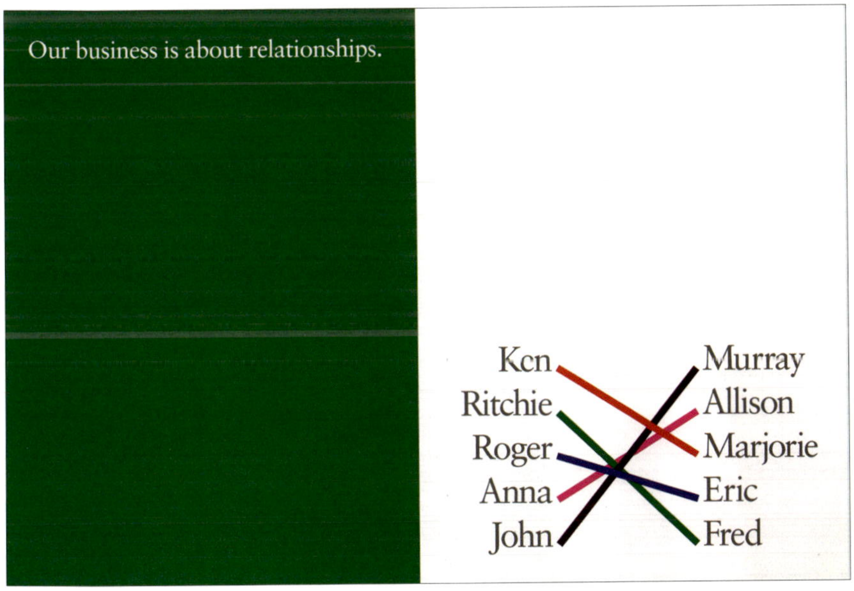

COVER PAPER 65lb. cougar opaque cover
TEXT PAPER 80lb. mccoy silk text
COLORS 6
PAGES 44
QUANTITY 30,000

Greater Bay Bancorp

FIRM_	cahan & associates
ART DIRECTORS_	bill cahan, michael braley
DESIGNER_	michael braley
PHOTOGRAPHER_	jock mcdonald
COPYWRITER_	thom elkjer
PRINTER_	anderson lithograph

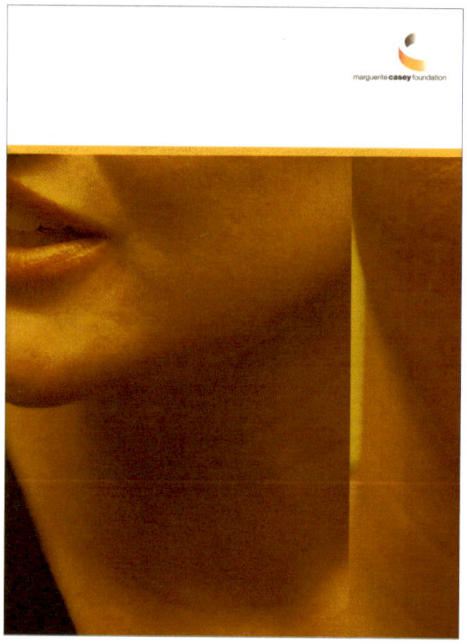

COVER PAPERS 100lb. Finch Fine Vanilla Cover; poster cover wrap on Foster Brights Gold
TEXT PAPER 100lb. Finch Fine Vanilla Text
COLORS 6
PAGES 32
QUANTITY 3,000

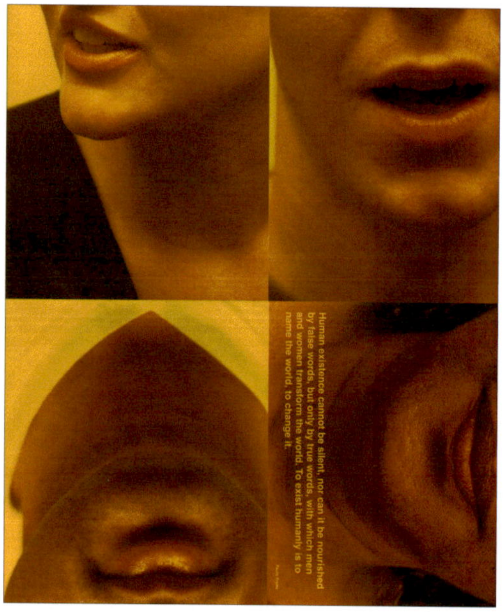

Marguerite Casey Foundation

FIRM_	Methodologie
ART DIRECTOR_	Anne Traver
DESIGNER_	Minh Nguyen
PHOTOGRAPHER_	Mary Jo McConahay, Young Lee, Kathleen King
COPYWRITER_	Mary Jo McConahay, David Brotherton
PRINTER_	Colorgraphics

COVER PAPER	65lb. sappi Lustro patina cover
TEXT PAPER	80lb. sappi Lustro patina text
COLORS	8
PAGES	60
QUANTITY	10,000

Simpletech

FIRM_	stoyan Design
ART DIRECTORS_	David stoyan wooters, Ryan Mahar
DESIGNER_	Ryan Mahar
PHOTOGRAPHER_	wendy Fletcher
PRINTER_	colorgraphics

COVER PAPER	80lb. utopia II Matte
TEXT PAPER	80lb. utopia II Matte
COLORS	7
PAGES	80
QUANTITY	25,000

Vivus Inc.

FIRM_	Howry Design Associates
ART DIRECTOR_	Jill Howry
DESIGNER_	Ty Whittington
PHOTOGRAPHER_	stock
PRINTER_	Waller Press

TEXT PAPER 150G. Luxosatin
PAGES 108
QUANTITY 5,000

Zumtobel AG

FIRM_	sagmeister Inc.
ART DIRECTOR_	stefan sagmeister
DESIGNER_	Matthias Ernstberger
PHOTOGRAPHER_	Bela Borsodi
COPYWRITER_	otto Riewoldt
PRINTERS_	veronaprint; cover: zumtobel staff, reiss international

Top 10 Photographed

{AWARD WINNER} {AWARD WINNER} {AWARD WINNER} {AWARD WINNER} {AWARD WINNER}

AW_ AW_ AW_ AW_ AW_

_AW _AW _AW _AW _AW

{AWARD WINNER} {AWARD WINNER} {AWARD WINNER} {AWARD WINNER} {AWARD WINNER}

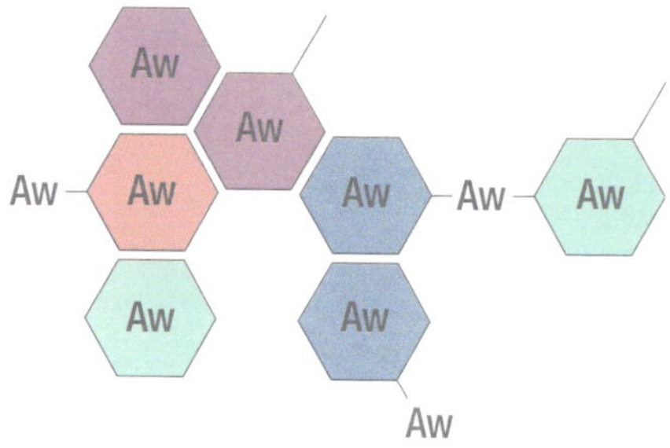

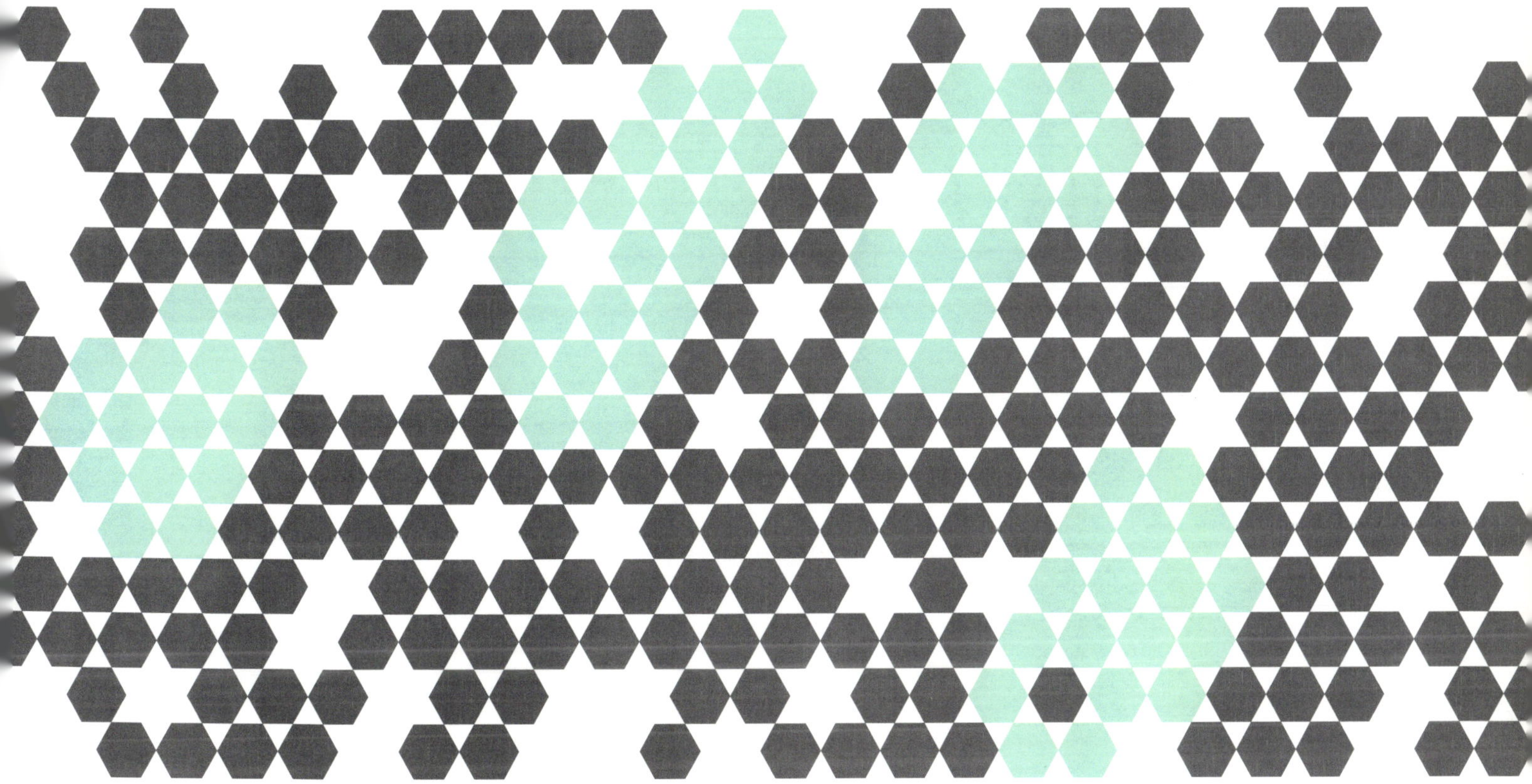

COVER PAPER 80lb. cougar opaque text
COLORS 5
PAGES 24
QUANTITY 2,000

Alberta Ballet

FIRM_ nu
ART DIRECTOR_ Monique Gamache
DESIGNER_ clay stang
PHOTOGRAPHER_ Daniel Gibbons
PRINTER_ sundog printing

COVER PAPER .013lb. fibermark touche
TEXT PAPER 100lb. Mohawk superfine text, 100lb. utopia one x silk text
COLORS 5
PAGES 54
QUANTITY 6,000

Alexandria Real Estate Equities, Inc.

FIRM_ OPTO Design
ART DIRECTORS_ john Klotnia, Brad simon
DESIGNERS_ Kelly Atkins, jennifer wenzlaff
ILLUSTRATORS_ jack unruh, Roger spears, Neil Armstrong, David wilcox, Peter Kramer, Tavis coburn, Nick Fasciano
PHOTOGRAPHERS_ eric staudenmaier, john Paul endress
PRINTER_ colorGraphics

COVER PAPER 80lb. cougar opaque text
TEXT PAPERS 60lb. fraser torchglow, 50lb. offset
COLORS 1
PAGES 12
QUANTITY 2,500

Calgary Exhibition & Stampede

FIRM_ Highwood communications Ltd.
ART DIRECTORS_ steve williams, keli pollock, Monique Gamache
DESIGNER_ Monique Gamache
PHOTOGRAPHER_ Jared sych
COPYWRITERS_ Nancy cope, Lindsey Galloway
PRINTERS_ calgary colorpress, sundog printing

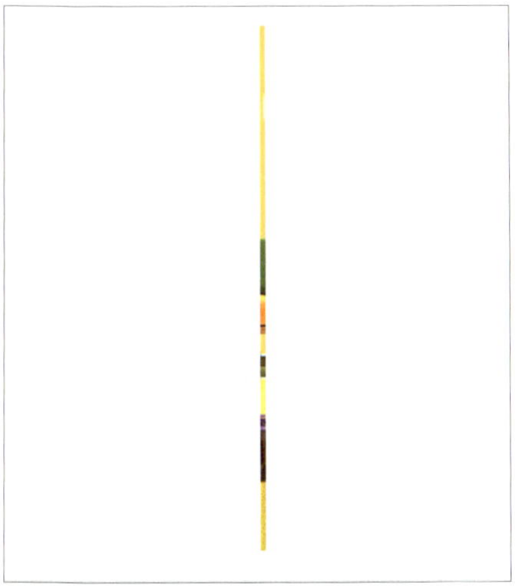

COVER PAPER 100lb. Sappi McCoy Matte Cover
TEXT PAPERS 100lb. Sappi McCoy Matte Text, 80lb. IP Via Pure White Vellum Text
COLORS 7
PAGES 102
QUANTITY 62,500

iStar Financial

FIRM_ Addison
ART DIRECTOR_ Richard Colbourne
DESIGNER_ Christina Antonopoulos
PHOTOGRAPHER_ Lorne Bridgman, Vincent Dixon
PRINTER_ Innovation Printing

In the 1950s housewives in the African American neighborhood of Gainesville, Georgia, started a social service club to collect money for funeral wreaths. Eventually the question loomed: "Why are so many of us dying?" Over the years the women of the Newtown Florist Club, located in a neighborhood described as "an industrial fallout zone," have become a force for environmental justice and against racism through legal challenges, lobbying, media coverage, and testing of toxic levels. Youngsters are being groomed as the next generation of grassroots leaders. Members still attend funerals together in community solidarity, bearing roses, wearing crisp white in summer, black in winter.

NEWTOWN FLORIST CLUB

GAINESVILLE
GEORGIA

The towers of a dog food processing mill loom above the children's playground, and backyards butt up against a scrap metal operation where machines crush cars, refrigerators, and smelly metal holding tanks. Factories chug and whirr, churning out chicken feed, hair spray, and chemically treated wood—they are closer to the neighborhood than schools. Park your car a few hours; you may return to find pale yellow grain dust covering it like a shroud.

"We got to talk about it," says Mozetta Whelchel, 77. She sits in an easy chair. Her sister Faye Bush, 67, lovingly runs a hand over Mozetta's head—hair is just beginning to grow in after an operation to remove a cancerous brain tumor. Mozetta's home, like the others on the quiet streets of Newtown, was built in the late 1930s to house the town's blacks after a killer tornado ripped through Gainesville. Many here blame sickness on the very air they breathe.

"No other person not of our race is going to come forward for us," says Faye, gently but plainly. "You have to do it yourself." Years after the African American homeowners had established their community, factories moved in. Today other parts of Gainesville are free of what is called "light industry." Northside residential neighborhoods unfold in quiet single-story homes or brick mansions, set on leafy lots that smell of honeysuckle, with no community-wide extraordinary health problems. The families of southside Newtown, meanwhile, suffer from lupus, an immune system disorder, and cancers, significantly out of proportion to their numbers. Soil and water runoff, they believe, has been contaminated over the years by industries which outsiders invited into their neighborhood.

For years, no one listened to their concerns.

Portrait of Mozetta Whelchel's daughter Moselee, who died of lupus at age 16.

COVER PAPERS	100lb. Finch Fine Vanilla cover; poster cover wrap on Foster Brights Gold
TEXT PAPER	100lb. Finch Fine Vanilla Text
COLORS	6
PAGES	32
QUANTITY	3,000

Marguerite Casey Foundation

FIRM_ Methodologie
ART DIRECTOR_ Anne Traver
DESIGNER_ Minh Nguyen
PHOTOGRAPHERS_ Mary Jo McConahay, Young Lee, Kathleen King
COPYWRITERS_ Mary Jo McConahay, David Brotherton
PRINTER_ Colorgraphics

COVER PAPER 300GSM GF Smith Zen Pure
TEXT PAPER 150GSM GF Smith Zen Pure
COLORS 5
PAGES 77
QUANTITY 25,000

MFI

FIRM_	SAS
ART DIRECTORS_	Andy Spencer, Gilmar Wendt, David Stocks
DESIGNERS_	Andy Spencer, Manja Hellpap
PHOTOGRAPHER_	Matt Stuart
COPYWRITER_	Martin Peacock
PRINTER_	Fulmar Colour Printing

COVER PAPER 60lb. Weyerhaeuser Cougar Text
TEXT PAPER 60lb. Weyerhaeuser Cougar Text
COLORS 8
PAGES 130
QUANTITY 15,000

Quiksilver

FIRM_ Stoyan Design
ART DIRECTORS_ David Stoyan Wooters, Chi Hang
DESIGNER_ Chi Hang
PHOTOGRAPHERS_ Various
PRINTER_ Colorgraphics

COVER PAPER Vent Nouvean
TEXT PAPER Vent Nouvean
COLORS 5
PAGES 128
QUANTITY 20,000

Samsung Group

FIRM_ The Corporate Agenda
ART DIRECTORS_ Chris Yun, Daniel Koh, Victor Rivera
PHOTOGRAPHERS_ Ashton Worthington, Leem Jun Bin
COPYWRITER_ Warren Berger
PRINTER_ Samsung Moonhwa Printing Company

COVER PAPER	80lb. utopia II Matte
TEXT PAPER	80lb. utopia II Matte
COLORS	7
PAGES	80
QUANTITY	25,000

Vivus

FIRM_	Howry Design Associates
ART DIRECTOR_	Jill Howry
DESIGNER_	Ty Whittington
PHOTOGRAPHER_	stock
PRINTER_	Waller Press

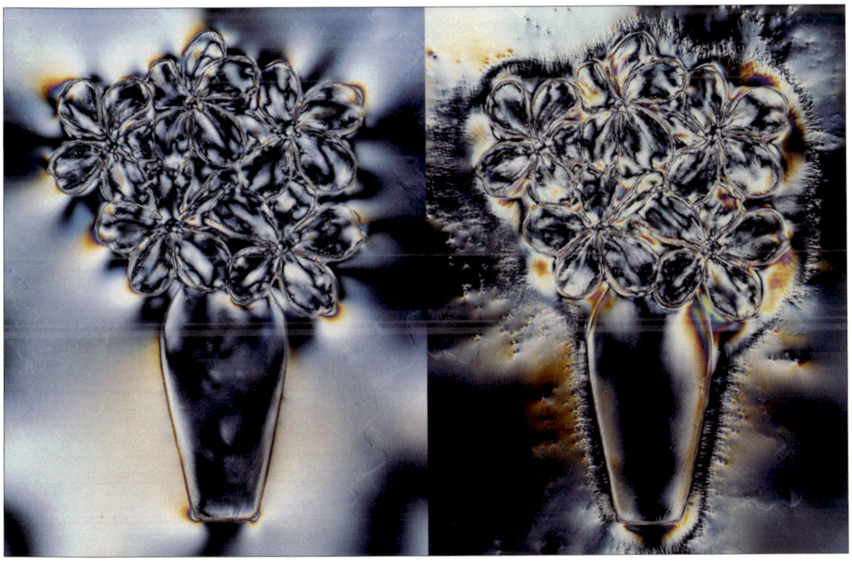

TEXT PAPER 150G. Luxosatin
COLORS 108
QUANTITY 5,000

Zumtobel AG

FIRM_ Sagmeister Inc.
ART DIRECTOR_ Stefan Sagmeister
DESIGNER_ Matthias Ernstberger
PHOTOGRAPHER_ Bela Borsodi
COPYWRITER_ Otto Riewoldt
PRINTERS_ Veronaprint; cover: Zumtobel staff, Reiss International

Top 10 Illustrated

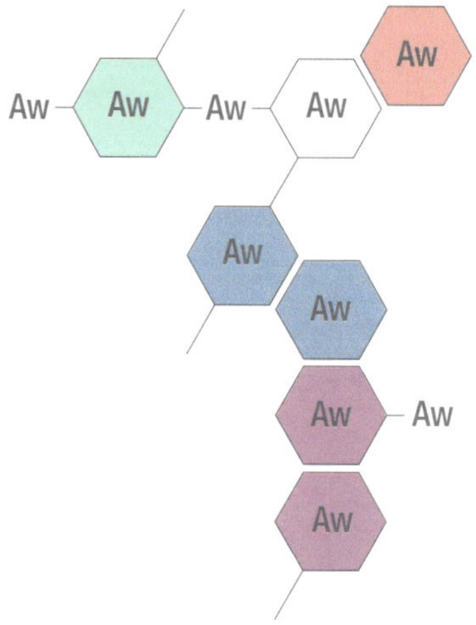

{AWARD WINNER} AW_
{AWARD WINNER} AW_
{AWARD WINNER} AW_
{AWARD WINNER} AW_
{AWARD WINNER} AW_

AW_ {AWARD WINNER}
AW_ {AWARD WINNER}
AW_ {AWARD WINNER}
AW_ {AWARD WINNER}
AW_ {AWARD WINNER}

COVER PAPER	.013lb. Fibermark Touche
TEXT PAPER	100lb. Mohawk Superfine Text, 100lb. Utopia One X Silk Text
COLORS	5
PAGES	54
QUANTITY	6,000

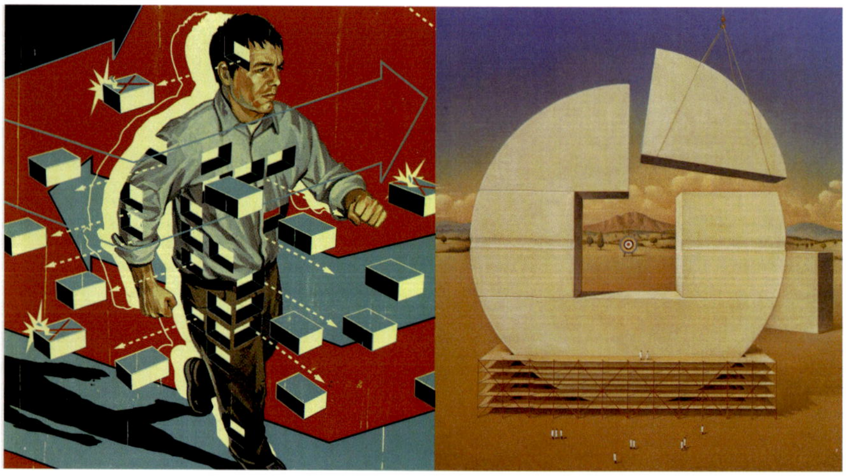

Alexandria Real Estate Equities, Inc.

FIRM_ Opto Design
ART DIRECTORS_ John Klotnia, Brad Simon
DESIGNERS_ Kelly Atkins, Jennifer Wenzlaff
ILLUSTRATORS_ Jack Unruh, Roger Spears, Neil Armstrong, David Wilcox, Peter Kramer, Tavis Coburn, Nick Fasciano
PHOTOGRAPHERS_ Eric Staudenmaier, John Paul Endress
PRINTER_ Colorgraphics

Coca-Cola Femsa

FIRM_	Paragraphs Design
ART DIRECTORS_	Meow Vatanatumrak, Rachel Radtke, Robin Zvonek
DESIGNER_	Meow Vatanatumrak
PHOTOGRAPHER_	Gabriel Covian
ILLUSTRATORS_	Peter Horjus, Fernando Andriacci
COPYWRITER_	Peter Warrick
PRINTER_	Quantum Color Graphics

COVER PAPER	100lb. Mohawk superfine ultrawhite eggshell cover
TEXT PAPERS	60lb. Mohawk superfine ultrawhite smooth cover, 70lb. Mohawk options warmwhite text
COLORS	7
PAGES	76
QUANTITY	10,000

COVER PAPERS 110lb. Nexfor Fraser Pegasus Brilliant White Super Smooth Cover

TEXT PAPER 100lb. Sappi McCoy Uncoated Text, 100lb. Nexfor Fraser Papers Pegasus Brilliant White Vellum Text

COLORS 8

PAGES 50

QUANTITY 10,000

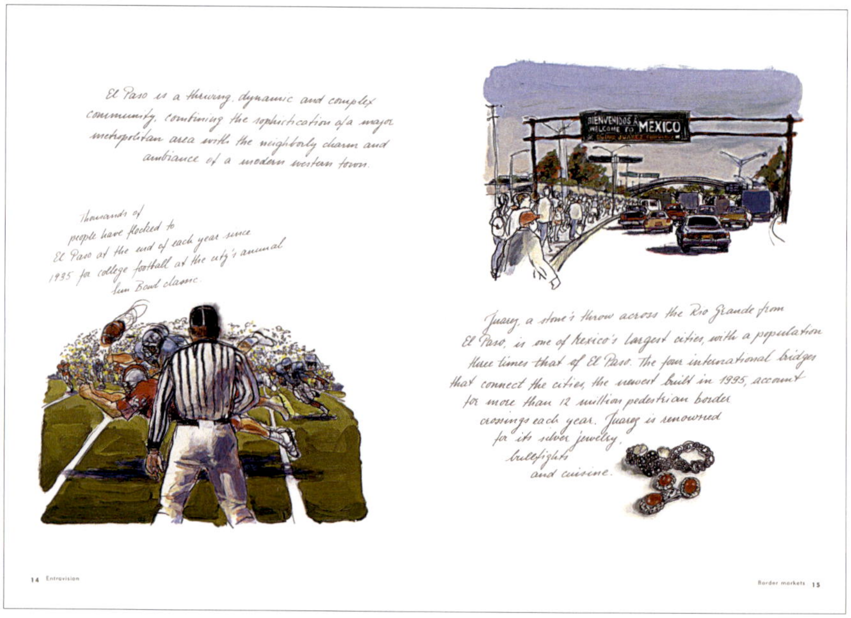

Entravision Communications

FIRM_	Douglas Joseph Partners
ART DIRECTOR_	Doug Joseph, Scott Lambert
DESIGNER_	Scott Lambert
ILLUSTRATORS_	Carol Fabricatore; Calligrapher: Elli Evertsen
COPYWRITER_	Larry Pearson
PRINTER_	Anderson Lithograph

First Data Corporation

FIRM_ VSA Partners
ART DIRECTORS_ Dana Arnett, Steve Ryan
DESIGNERS_ Steve Ryan, Luke Galambos
ILLUSTRATOR_ Istvan Banyai
COPYWRITER_ Mike Noble
PRINTER_ Hennegan

COVER PAPER 80lb. Mohawk options warm white smooth cover
TEXT PAPERS 80lb. Mohawk satin warm white smooth text, 60lb. Mohawk satin warm white smooth text
COLORS 7
PAGES 92
QUANTITY 300,000

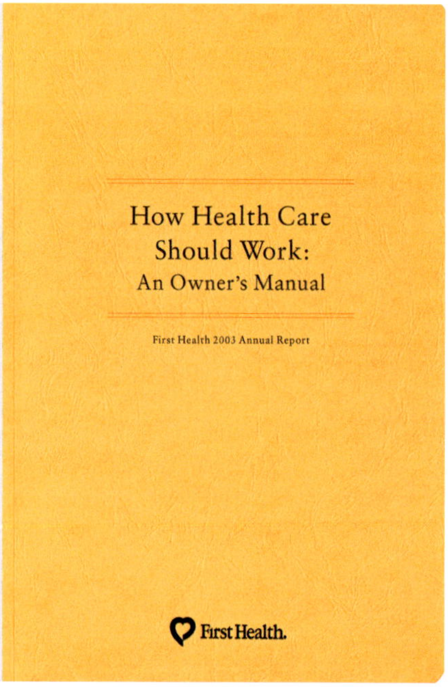

COVER PAPER 80lb. Fibermark, Leatherette Jersey Cover
TEXT PAPERS 70lb. Domtar Whitehall Smooth Text, 80lb. Scheufelen North America, Inc. Gleneagle Gloss Text
COLORS 3
PAGES 152
QUANTITY 33,150

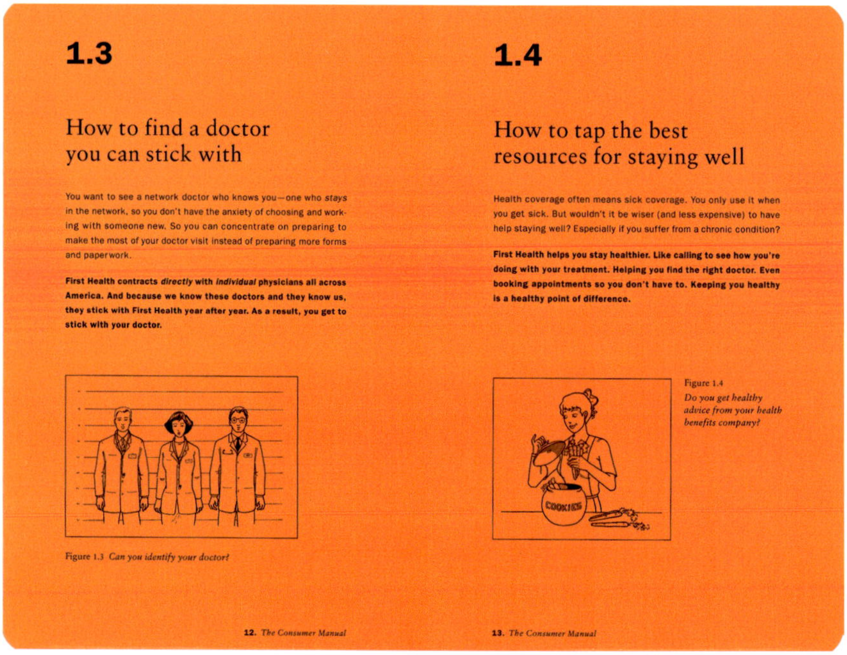

1.3

How to find a doctor you can stick with

You want to see a network doctor who knows you—one who *stays* in the network, so you don't have the anxiety of choosing and working with someone new. So you can concentrate on preparing to make the most of your doctor visit instead of preparing more forms and paperwork.

First Health contracts *directly* with *individual* physicians all across America. And because we know these doctors and they know us, they stick with First Health year after year. As a result, you get to stick with your doctor.

Figure 1.3 *Can you identify your doctor?*

1.4

How to tap the best resources for staying well

Health coverage often means sick coverage. You only use it when you get sick. But wouldn't it be wiser (and less expensive) to have help staying well? Especially if you suffer from a chronic condition?

First Health helps you stay healthier. Like calling to see how you're doing with your treatment. Helping you find the right doctor. Even booking appointments so you don't have to. Keeping you healthy is a healthy point of difference.

Figure 1.4
Do you get healthy advice from your health benefits company?

12. *The Consumer Manual*
13. *The Consumer Manual*

First Health

FIRM_	Petrick Design
ART DIRECTOR_	Robert Petrick
DESIGNER_	Tracy West
ILLUSTRATOR_	Brenda Brown
COPYWRITER_	Bruce Hetrick
PRINTER_	Lake County Press

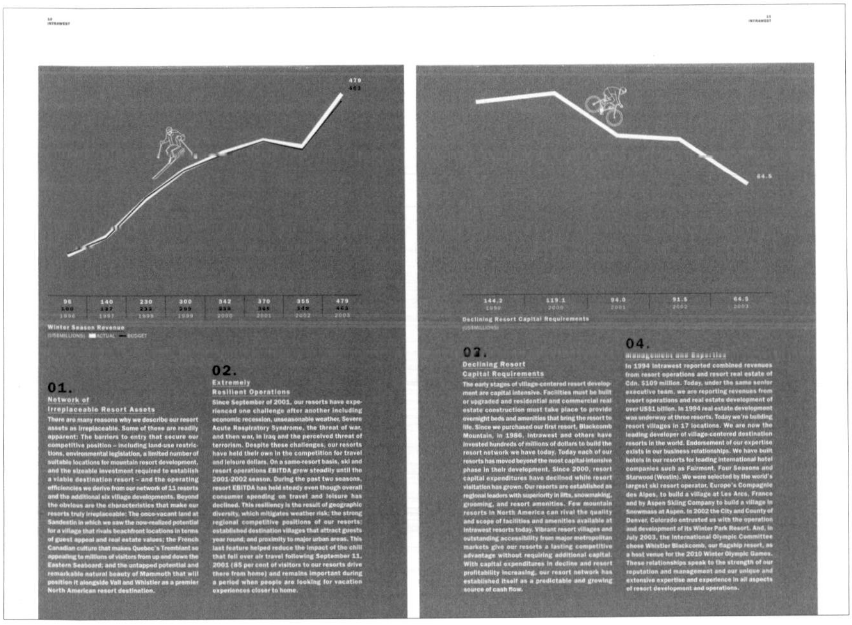

Intrawest Corporation

FIRM_ samatamason
ART DIRECTORS_ Dave Mason, Pamela Lee
DESIGNERS_ Pamela Lee, Keith Leinweber
PHOTOGRAPHERS_ various
ILLUSTRATOR_ Keith Leinweber
PRINTER_ Blanchette Press

COVER PAPER 80lb. Fraser papers Pegasus vellum cover
TEXT PAPERS 70lb. Fraser papers Pegasus vellum text, 80lb. Domtar Luna silk text
COLORS 7
PAGES 64
QUANTITY 25,000

COVER PAPER	100lb. spicers paper endevour matt cover
TEXT PAPER	100lb. spicers paper endevour text
COLORS	6
PAGES	62
QUANTITY	15,000

Mentor Corporation

FIRM_	McNulty & Company
ART DIRECTORS_	Eugene Bustillos, Richard Huvard
DESIGNERS_	Eugene Bustillos, Ryan Plantin
ILLUSTRATORS_	Gavin Reece, Alexis Brandon
COPYWRITER_	Richard Huvard
PRINTER_	Colorgraphics

COVER PAPER	100lb. Glacier Opaque Text
TEXT PAPER	100lb. Glacier Opaque Text
COLORS	6
PAGES	40
QUANTITY	2,500

PEN Canada

FIRM_	Soapbox Design Communications Inc.
ART DIRECTOR_	Gary Beelik
DESIGNER_	Jim Ryce
ILLUSTRATOR_	Luba Lukova
COPYWRITER_	Bert Archer
PRINTER_	Sumerset Graphics Ltd.

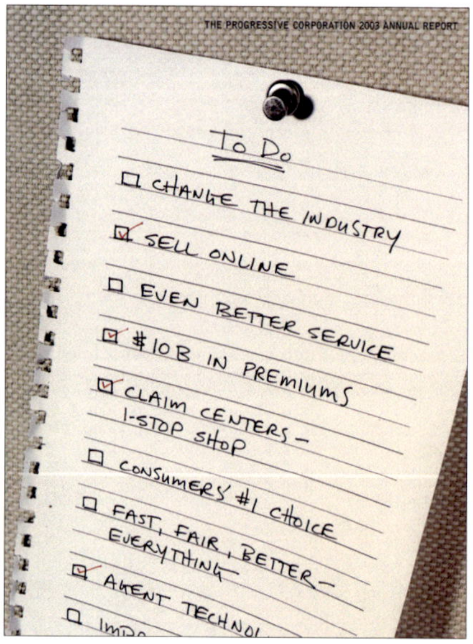

COVER PAPER	100lb. french smart white cover
TEXT PAPER	100lb. french smart white text, 70lb. french construction cement green text, 70lb. french construction slate blue text
COLORS	7
PAGES	38
QUANTITY	55,000

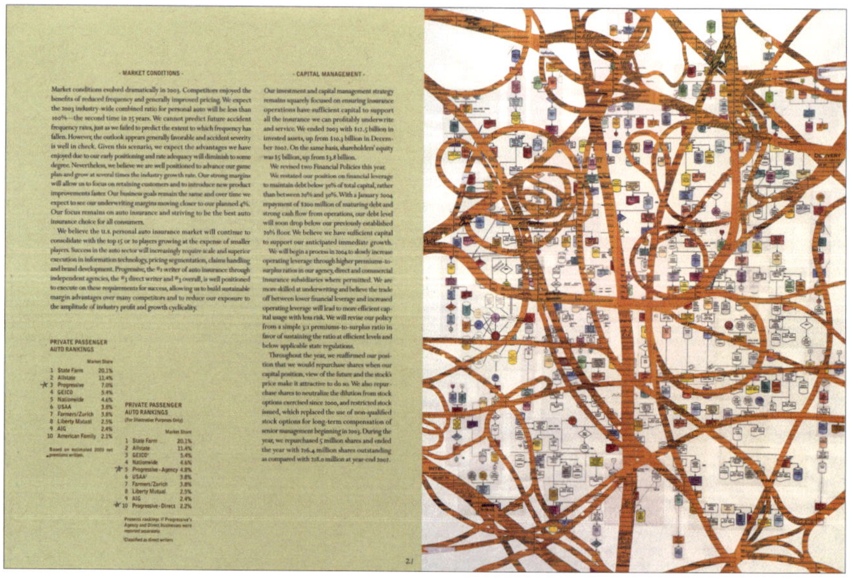

The Progressive Corporation

FIRM_	Nesnadny + Schwartz: Cleveland + New York + Toronto
ART DIRECTORS_	Joyce Nesnadny, Mark Schwartz
DESIGNERS_	Joyce Nesnadny, Michelle Moehler, Keith Pishnery
ARTIST_	Carlos Vega
COPYWRITER_	Glenn Renwick - The Progressive Corporation
PRINTER_	Fortran Printing

COVER PAPER 70lb. Finch opaque creme text
TEXT PAPER 70lb. Finch opaque creme smooth
COLORS 2
PAGES 32
QUANTITY 1,500

Turn Around

FIRM_ Spur Design
ART DIRECTOR_ David Plunkert
DESIGNERS_ Kurt Seidle, David Plurkert
ILLUSTRATOR_ David Plunkert
COPYWRITER_ Shelly Apple - Terranova
PRINTER_ Advance Printing

Top

10 Typography

AW_ {AWARD WINNER}
AW_ {AWARD WINNER}
AW_ {AWARD WINNER}
AW_ {AWARD WINNER}
AW_ {AWARD WINNER}

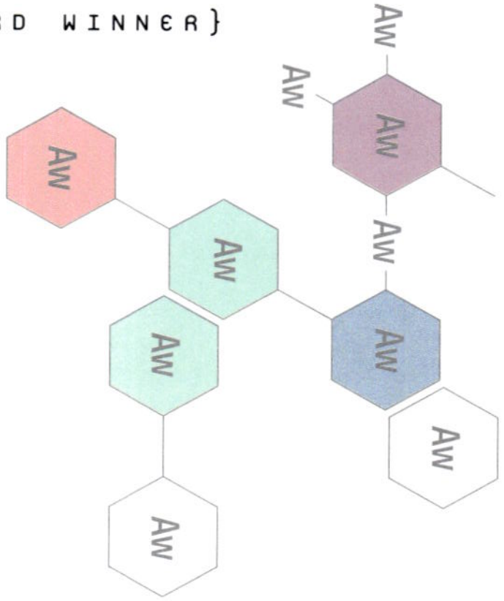

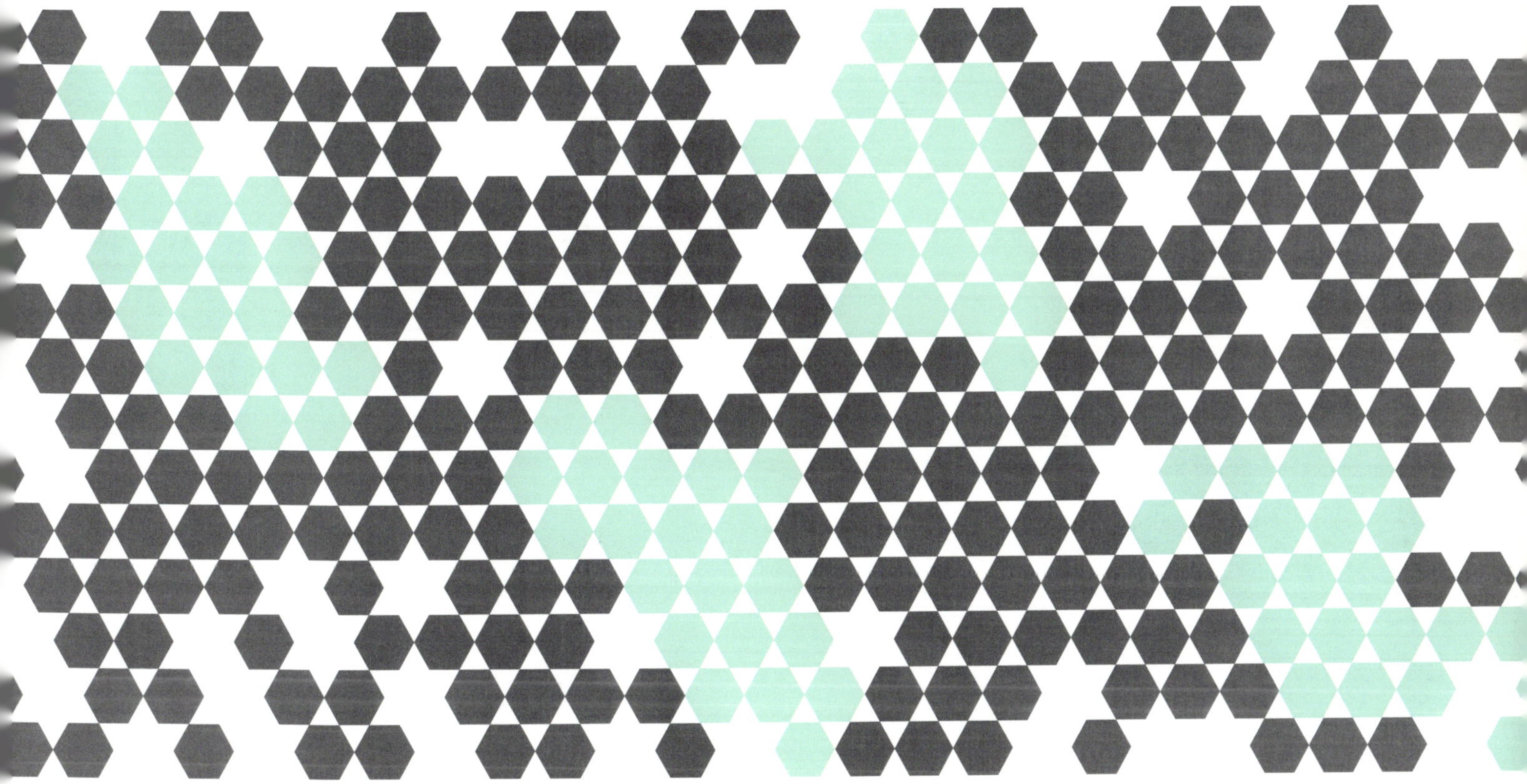

COVER PAPER 80lb. Fraser Pegasus Black cover
TEXT PAPERS 80lb. smooth text Fraser Pegasus Museum White, 100lb. Domtar Luna Gloss White
COLORS 6
PAGES 82
QUANTITY 3,000

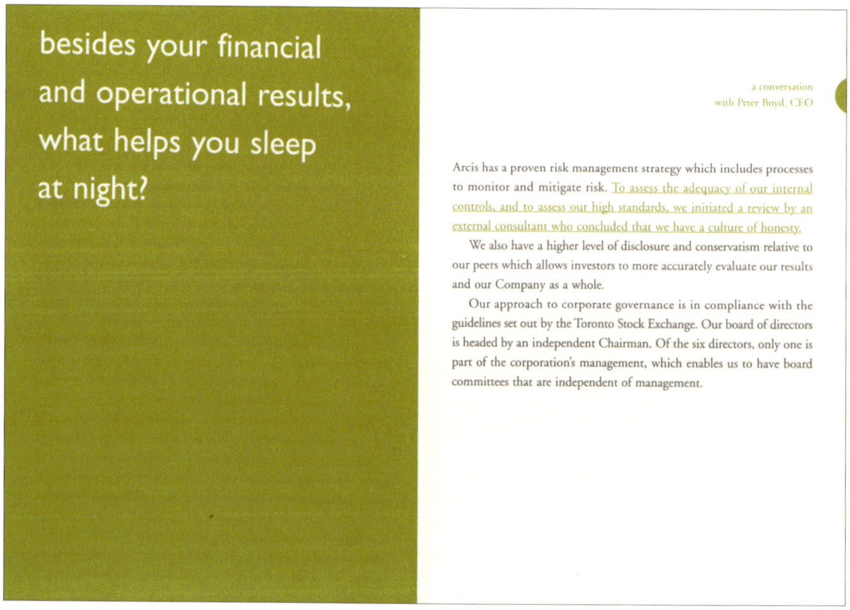

Arcis Corporation

FIRM_ SagesWright Inc.
ART DIRECTOR_ Rita Sasges
DESIGNERS_ Rita Sasges, Isabel Abdai
PHOTOGRAPHERS_ Gerrard Yunker, Phillip Dykes
COPYWRITER_ National PR
PRINTER_ Blanchette Press

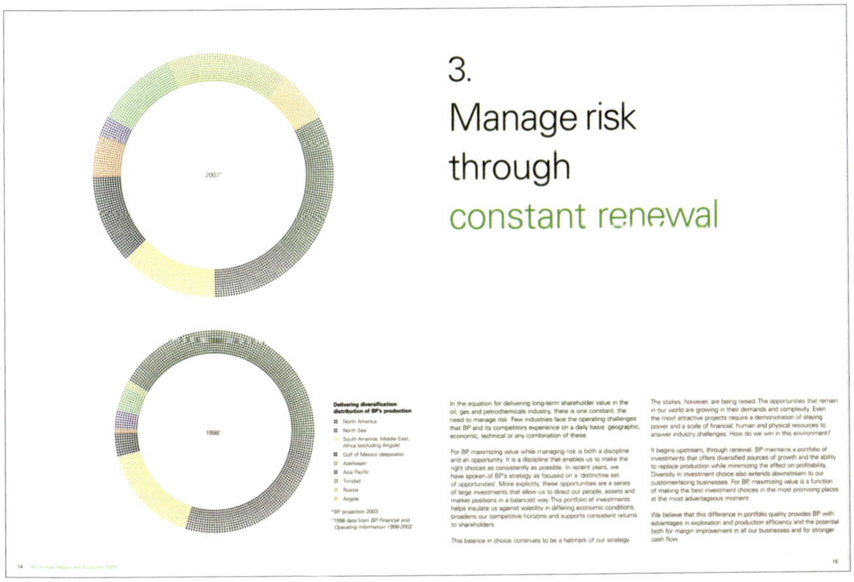

COVER PAPER	80lb. Mohawk options 100% PC white
TEXT PAPER	80lb. Mohawk options 100% PC white
COLORS	8
PAGES	120
QUANTITY	126,000

BP

FIRM_	VSA Partners
ART DIRECTORS_	Dana Arnett, Jamie Koval
DESIGNERS_	Dan Knuckey, Brock Conrad
PHOTOGRAPHERS_	Various
COPYWRITER_	Andy Blankenburg
PRINTERS_	Sandy Alexander, St. Ives Burrups

COVER PAPER .088 Board casebound black pearl linen
TEXT PAPERS 100lb. Sappi McCoy Matte Text, 80lb. Mohawk Warm White Vellum Text
COLORS 8
PAGES 86
QUANTITY 10,000

Courier Corporation

FIRM_	Weymouth Design
ART DIRECTOR_	Robert Krivicich
DESIGNER_	Aaron Haesaert
PHOTOGRAPHER_	Michael Weymouth
COPYWRITER_	John Temple
PRINTER_	Quebecor World Acme

COVER PAPER	65lb. cougar opaque cover
TEXT PAPER	80lb. Mccoy silk text
COLORS	6
PAGES	44
QUANTITY	30,000

Greater Bay Bancorp

FIRM_	Cahan & Associates
ART DIRECTORS_	Bill Cahan, Michael Braley
DESIGNER_	Michael Braley
PHOTOGRAPHER_	Jock McDonald
COPYWRITER_	Thom Elkjer
PRINTER_	Anderson Lithograph

COVER PAPER 80lb. Fox River Sundance Ultra White Smooth Cover
TEXT PAPER 80lb. Fox River Sundance Ultra White Smooth Text
COLORS 6
PAGES 98
QUANTITY 425,000

GROW VALUE and STRENGTHEN the BRAND

LEAVING *well enough* ALONE
JUST ISN'T *in our* NATURE

To be sure, we left well enough alone when we retained the character that's been part of the Sportster soul since 1957. But don't be fooled. From the fender-tip to fender-tip redesign of the Sportster motorcycle family, to the street-fighter personality of the Buell XBs, or the dozens of innovations across the entire product line, Harley-Davidson lives to bring newer and better products to market. Even if they come disguised as tradition.

First and foremost, we're a motorcycle company. So when we talk about growing value, motorcycles are not only king, they are key to keeping the faith among the faithful and turning dreamers into the newest members of the family.

In just the last five years, we've brought more innovation to market—like the Twin Cam 88® and Twin Cam 88B™ power plants and the V-Rod motorcycle—more quickly and with more success than at any other time in our history. In short, we've redesigned all product families and given birth to a new one. The re-engineered Sportster is just the latest example of how we innovate and listen to riders. Each innovation, every refinement, is made with an eye on making a great thing even better. And every change, large or small, is executed in the unique and purposeful Harley-Davidson way that has brought the Company to where it is today.

Now that we've expanded the cutting-edge facilities at the Willie G. Davidson Product Development Center and added system capacity through our new Softail plant, Harley-Davidson stands poised to leverage these investments. Hold on to your helmets. We're just getting started.

PHOTOGRAPH
FACING PAGE: *The 2004 Sportster motorcycles improve rider ergonomics and enhance the signature Sportster look through cleaner styling. Sportster® 1200 Custom*

BUELL:
{NEW *for* 2004}
RIGHT: 2004 Buell® Lightning® XB12S, *pictured in Racing Red*
LEFT: 2004 Buell® Firebolt® XB12R, *pictured in Midnight Black*

PAGE 19

Harley-Davidson

FIRM_	VSA Partners
ART DIRECTOR_	Jason Jones
DESIGNER_	Jacob Gardner
PHOTOGRAPHER_	Charlie Simokaitis
COPYWRITERS_	Bob Klein, Harley-Davidson
PRINTER_	Litho, Inc.

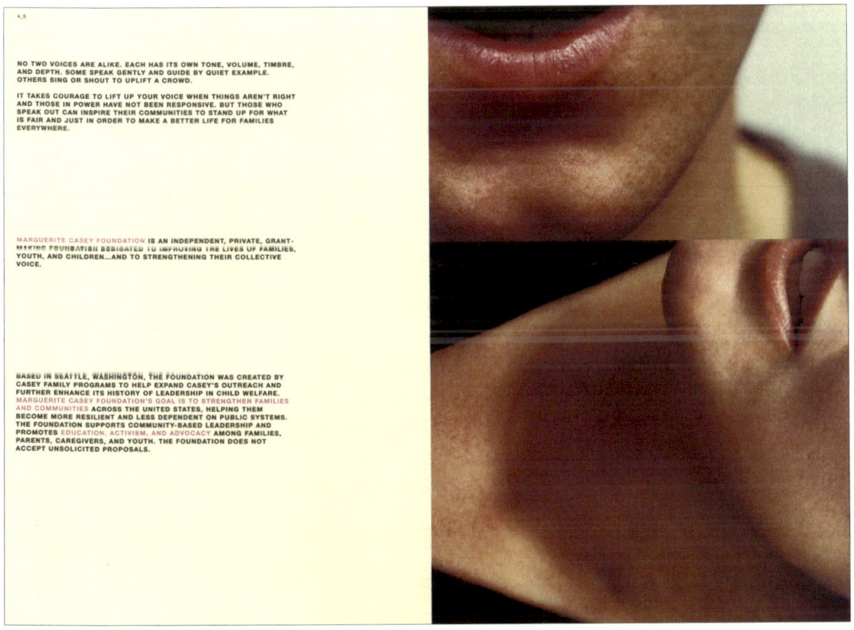

Marguerite Casey Foundation

FIRM_	Methodologie
ART DIRECTOR_	Anne Traver
DESIGNER_	Minh Nguyen
PHOTOGRAPHERS	Mary Jo McConahay, Young Lee, Kathleen King
COPYWRITERS_	Mary Jo McConahay, David Brotherton
PRINTER_	Colorgraphics

COVER PAPERS	100lb. Finch Fine Vanilla cover; poster cover wrap on Foster Brights Gold
TEXT PAPER	100lb. Finch Fine Vanilla text
COLORS	6
PAGES	32
QUANTITY	3,000

COVER PAPER 65lb. Utopia 2 White Matte Cover
TEXT PAPER 70lb. Utopia 2 White Matte Text
COLORS 8
PAGES 32
QUANTITY 8,500

Neoforma

FIRM_	Cahan & Associates
ART DIRECTORS_	Bill Cahan, Sharrie Brooks
DESIGNER_	Sharrie Brooks
PHOTOGRAPHERS_	Graham MacIndoe, Sian Kennedy
COPYWRITER_	Kathy Cooper Parker
PRINTER_	Anderson Lithograph

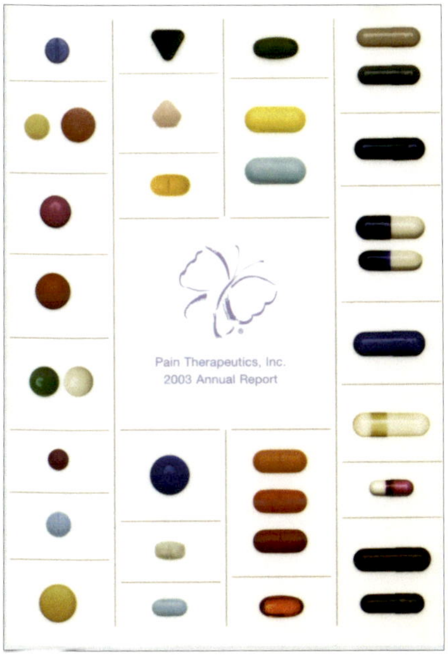

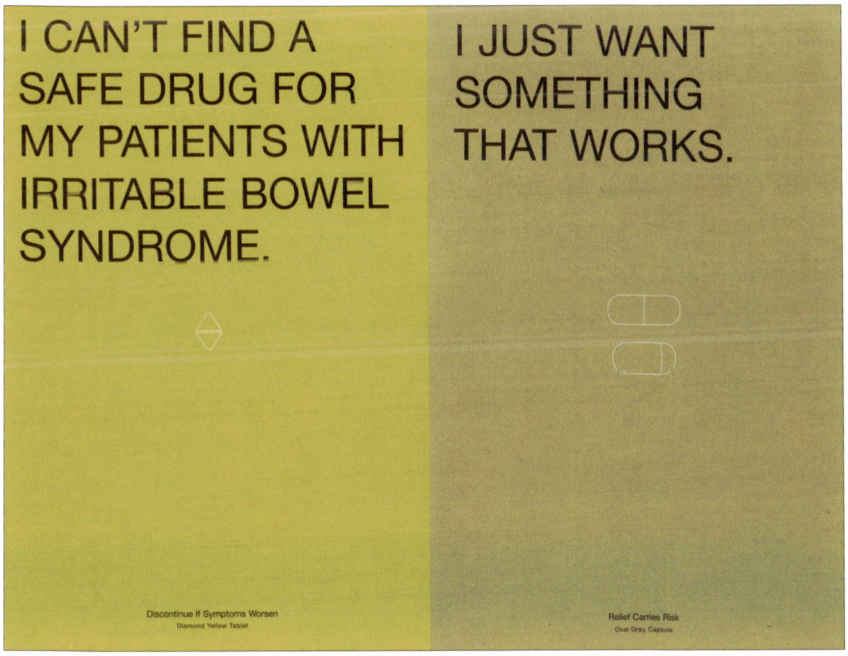

COVER PAPER 130lb. McCoy silk cover
TEXT PAPER 100lb. McCoy silk text, 62lb. Yupo translucent text
COLORS 9
PAGES 48
QUANTITY 3,000

Pain Therapeutics

FIRM_ Howry Design Associates
ART DIRECTOR_ Jill Howry
DESIGNER_ Todd Richards
ILLUSTRATOR_ Liisa Turan
PRINTER_ Color Graphics

COVER PAPER 100lb. Glacier opaque text
TEXT PAPER 100lb. Glacier opaque text
COLORS 6
PAGES 40
QUANTITY 2,500

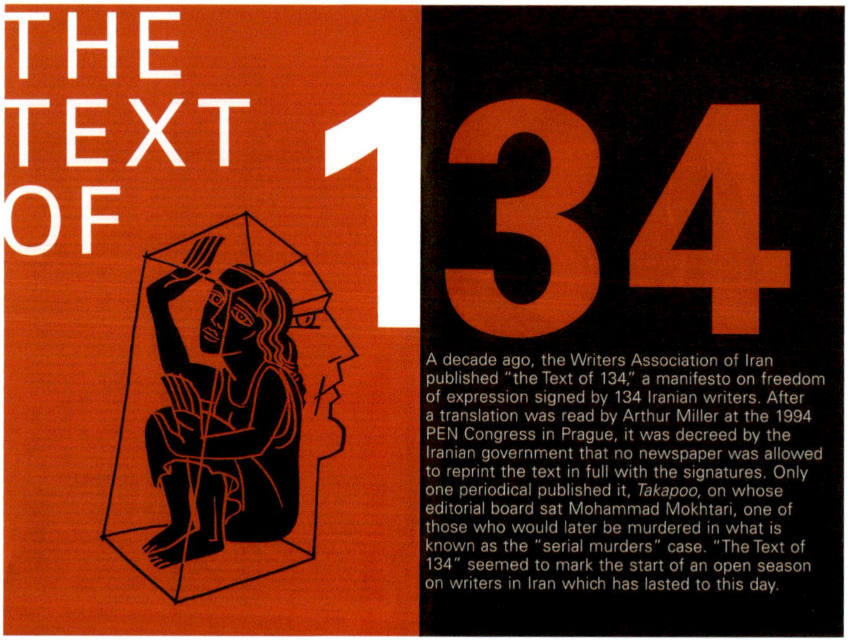

PEN Canada

FIRM_	Soapbox Design Communications Inc.
ART DIRECTOR_	Gary Beelik
DESIGNER_	Jim Ryce
ILLUSTRATOR_	Luba Lukova
COPYWRITER_	Bert Archer
PRINTER_	Sumerset Graphics Ltd.

Silicon Valley Bancshares
2003 Annual Report

While growing its product offering, Alliant delivered on its nationwide strategy to expand into key markets in which Silicon Valley Bank has an established presence. This past year Alliant opened its first technology-focused regional office in the Boston area.

While its financial performance in 2003 was disappointing, Alliant has taken decisive action to correct the situation, strengthening its leadership network and improving the referral and cross-selling synergies between itself and Silicon Valley Bank.

In 2003, we undertook a meaningful expansion of our Merchant Bank, broadening our target market to include relationships with the entire scope of private equity firms and funds. With more than a dozen seasoned professionals across the country calling on this market,

Alliant significantly enhanced its core service offering with the launch of its Private Capital Group. Focused on providing advisory services for the private placement of securities, Alliant's Private Capital Group complements its M&A advisory business, offering clients the flexibility of financing or sale, depending on their specific needs.

we've already seen considerable traction in leveraging our venture services expertise into new private equity partnerships.

Our own limited partnerships—SVB Strategic Investors Fund, L.P. and Silicon Valley BancVentures, L.P.—continued to perform within their expected ranges in 2003. Going forward, we anticipate continued growth of our merchant banking activities through enhanced fund management capabilities and the addition of new proprietary funds.

Going Global

Having already penetrated all major technology and life science markets in the United States, Silicon Valley Bancshares' global expansion has now become a central component of our ongoing growth initiative and long-term strategy.

In 2003, we undertook a meaningful expansion of our Merchant Bank, broadening our target market to include relationships with the entire scope of private equity firms and funds.

COVER PAPER 65lb. cougar opaque cover
TEXT PAPER 80lb. Mccoy silk text
COLORS 4
PAGES 146

Silicon Valley Bank

FIRM_ Cahan & Associates
ART DIRECTORS_ Bill Cahan, Michael Braley
DESIGNER_ Michael Braley
PRINTER_ Anderson Lithograph

Top 10 Printed

{AWARD WINNER}
{AWARD WINNER}
{AWARD WINNER}
{AWARD WINNER}
{AWARD WINNER}

AW_
AW_
AW_
AW_
AW_

_AW
_AW
_AW
_AW
_AW

{AWARD WINNER}
{AWARD WINNER}
{AWARD WINNER}
{AWARD WINNER}
{AWARD WINNER}

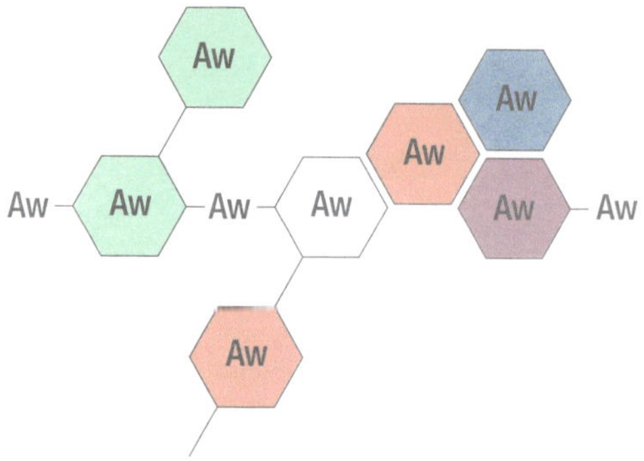

COVER PAPER weyerhauser cougar opaque cover
TEXT PAPER weyerhauser cougar opaque text
COLORS 6
PAGES 90
QUANTITY 150,000

Burlington Northern Santa Fe

FIRM_ Methodologie
ART DIRECTORS_ Janet DeDonato, Dale Hart
DESIGNER_ Royal Stuart
PHOTOGRAPHER_ Eric Myer
COPYWRITER_ Hugh Saffel
PRINTER_ Williamson Printing

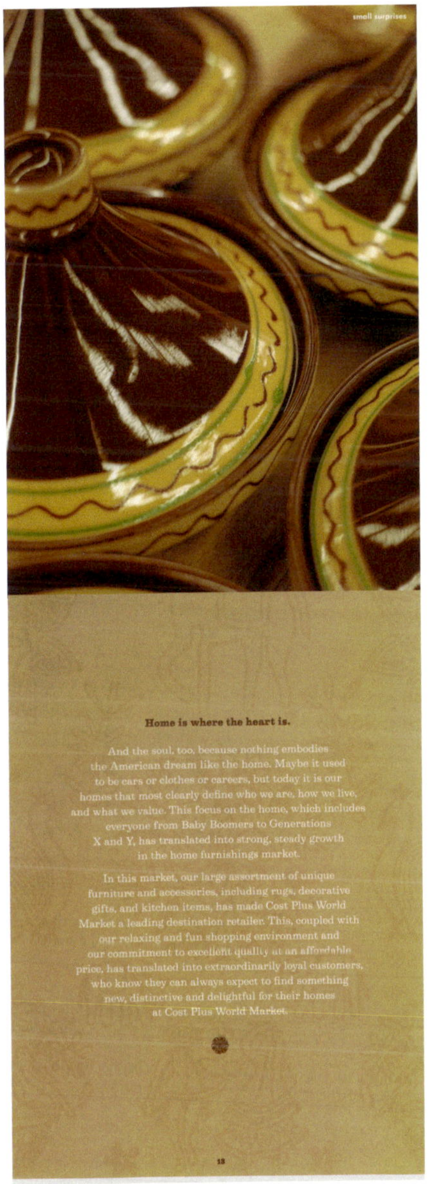

COVER PAPER	80lb. Fox River confetti
TEXT PAPER	65lb. Mohawk options
COLORS	5
PAGES	51
QUANTITY	11,000

Cost Plus World Market

FIRM_	Turner & Associates
ART DIRECTOR_	Steve Turner
DESIGNER_	Laura Milton
PHOTOGRAPHERS_	Angie Wyant, Jock McDonald
COPYWRITER_	Terry London
PRINTER_	Watermark Press

COVER PAPER .088 Board casebound Black pearl Linen
TEXT PAPERS 100lb. Sappi Mccoy Matte Text, 80lb. Mohawk Warm White Vellum Text
COLORS 8
PAGES 86
QUANTITY 10,000

Courier Corporartion

FIRM_	Weymouth Design
ART DIRECTOR_	Robert Krivicich
DESIGNER_	Aaron Haesaert
PHOTOGRAPHER_	Michael Weymouth
COPYWRITER_	John Temple
PRINTER_	Quebecor World Acme

COVER PAPER 140lb. French Muscletone Black cover

TEXT PAPER 100lb. Appleton Utopia One X Xtra Bright Silk Text, 60lb. French Durotone Primer Gold Text, 80lb. French Durotone Packing Box Board Text

COLORS 5

PAGES 50

QUANTITY 3,500

The George Gund Foundation

FIRM_ Nesnadny + Schwartz, Cleveland + New York + Toronto

ART DIRECTOR_ Mark Schwartz

DESIGNERS_ Michelle Moehler, Joyce Nesnadny

PHOTOGRAPHER_ Andrew Borowiec

COPYWRITERS_ Geoffrey Gund, David Abbott, Deena Epstein

PRINTER_ Fortran Printing

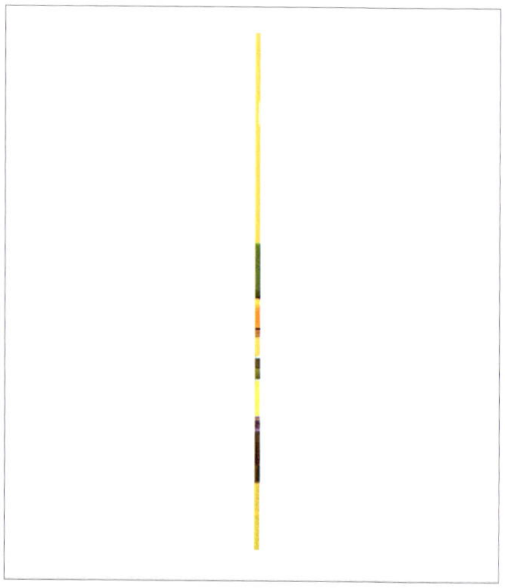

COVER PAPER 100lb. sappi Mccoy Matte cover
TEXT PAPERS 100lb. sappi Mccoy Matte text, 80lb. LP Via pure white vellum text
COLORS 7
PAGES 102
QUANTITY 62,500

iStar Financial

FIRM_ Addison
ART DIRECTOR_ Richard Colbourne
DESIGNER_ Christina Antonopoulos
PHOTOGRAPHERS_ Lorne Bridgman, Vincent Dixon
PRINTER_ Innovation Printing

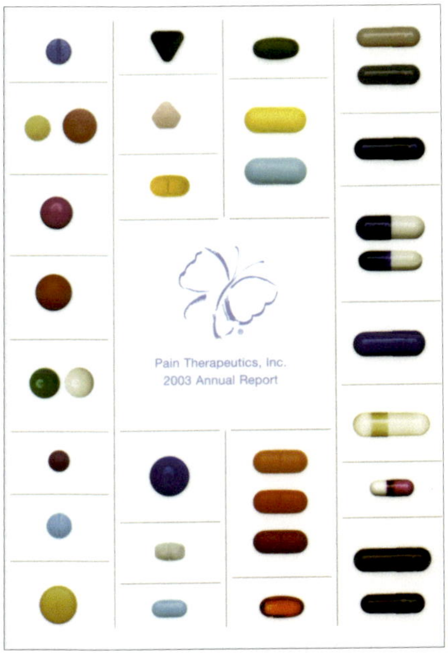

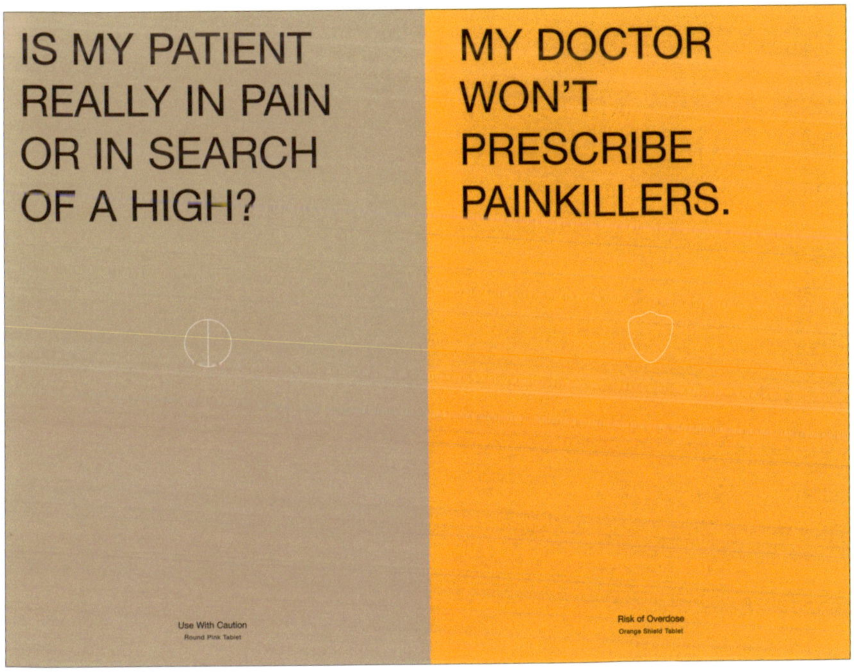

COVER PAPER 130lb. McCoy silk cover
TEXT PAPERS 100lb. McCoy silk text, 62lb. yupo translucent text
COLORS 9
PAGES 48
QUANTITY 3,000

Pain Therapeutics

FIRM_ Howry Design Associates
ART DIRECTOR_ Jill Howry
DESIGNER_ Todd Richards
ILLUSTRATOR_ Liisa Turan
PRINTER_ Color Graphics

COVER PAPER 60lb. Weyerhaeuser Cougar Text
TEXT PAPER 60lb. Weyerhaeuser Cougar Text
COLORS 8
PAGES 130
QUANTITY 15,000

Quiksilver

FIRM_ Stoyan Design
ART DIRECTORS_ David Stoyan Wooters, Chi Hang
DESIGNER_ Chi Hang
PHOTOGRAPHERS_ various
PRINTER_ Colorgraphics

COVER PAPER vent nouvean
TEXT PAPER vent nouvean
COLORS 5
PAGES 128
QUANTITY 20,000

Samsung Group

FIRM_ the corporate agenda
ART DIRECTORS_ chris yun, daniel koh, victor rivera
PHOTOGRAPHERS_ ashton worthington, leem jun bin
COPYWRITER_ warren berger
PRINTER_ samsung moonhwa printing company

COVER PAPER 80lb. cougar smooth cover
TEXT PAPERS 65lb. cougar smooth cover, 60lb. Lynx smooth book
COLORS 4
PAGES 28
QUANTITY 30,000

SPCA of Texas

FIRM_ RBMM
ART DIRECTORS_ Steve Gibbs, Dick Mitchell, Brian Boyd
DESIGNER_ Brian Owens
ILLUSTRATOR_ David Vaught
PHOTOGRAPHERS_ Peter Kao (cover), Joe Grisham, Chris Whalen, Mark Bumgarner, John Wong, Robie Capps, Tadd Myers, Heather Ezell
COPYWRITERS_ David Culp, Kathy Edwards
PRINTER_ Williamson Printing Corporation

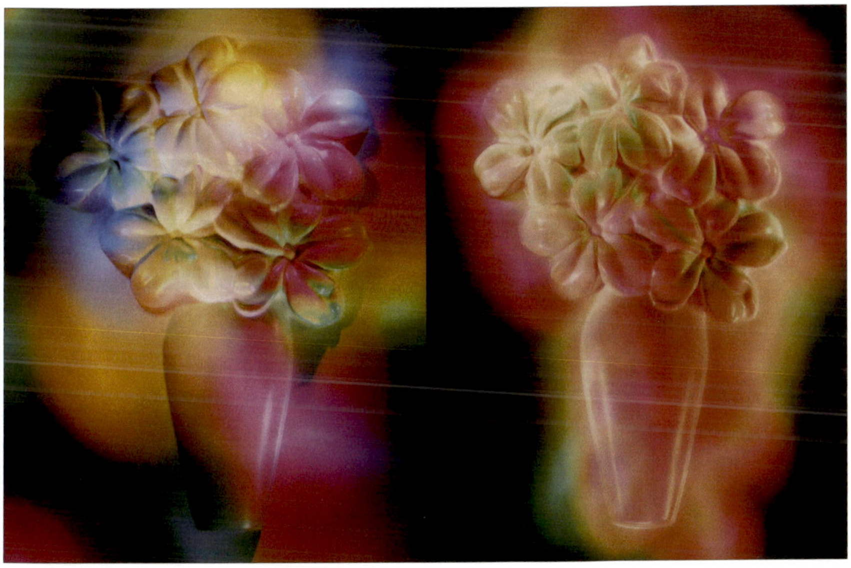

TEXT PAPER 150G. Luxosatin
PAGES 108
QUANTITY 5,000

Zumtobel AG

FIRM_ sagmeister Inc.
ART DIRECTOR stefan sagmeister
DESIGNER_ Matthias Ernstberger
PHOTOGRAPHER_ Bela Borsodi
COPYWRITER_ otto Riewoldt
PRINTERS_ veronaprint; cover: zumtobel staff, reiss international

19 AR 100

{GOALS}	GO_	PE_	{PERSEVERANCE}
{IMAGINATION}	IM_	SW_	{SWEAT}
{MESSAGE}	ME_	DE_	{DESIRE}
{INSIGHT}	IN_	CO_	{COFFEE}
{AUDIENCE}	AU_	EX_	{EXPLORATION}

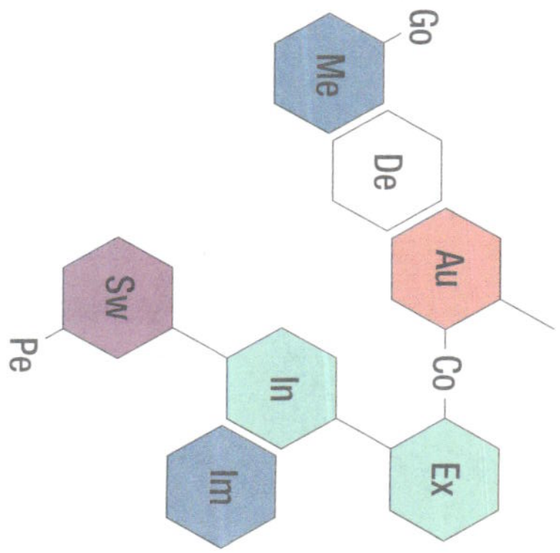

100

Aber Diamond Corporation

FIRM_ the works design communications ltd.
ART DIRECTOR_ scott mcfarland
DESIGNER_ nelson silva
PHOTOGRAPHER_ mathew plexman
ILLUSTRATOR_ john jinks
COPYWRITERS_ eric johnson, marla gale
PRINTER_ somerset graphics

COVER PAPER 110lb. synergy felt cover pure white
TEXT PAPERS 100lb. synergy felt text, 80lb. synergy felt text
COLORS 8
PAGES 64
QUANTITY 15 million

COVER PAPER centura
TEXT PAPER centura
COLORS 9
PAGES 38
QUANTITY 90,000

Adobe Systems, Inc.

FIRM_ MetaDesign
ART DIRECTOR_ Brett Wickens
DESIGNER_ Julian Bittiner
PHOTOGRAPHERS_ Todd Hido, Martin Evening, Karen Nichols, Steven Underwood
ILLUSTRATORS_ Peter Saville, Howard Wakefield; Deutsch, Inc.; The Orphanage
COPYWRITER_ Jay O'Rear
PRINTER_ Anderson Lithograph

FIRM_ nu
ART DIRECTOR_ monique gamache
PHOTOGRAPHER_ clay stang
COPYWRITER_ daniel gibbons
PRINTER_ sundog printing

Alberta Ballet

COVER PAPER 80lb. cougar opaque text
COLORS 5
PAGES 24
QUANTITY 2,000

COVER PAPER .013lb. fibermark touche
TEXT PAPERS 100lb. mohawk superfine text, 100lb. utopia one x silk text
COLORS 5
PAGES 54
QUANTITY 6,000

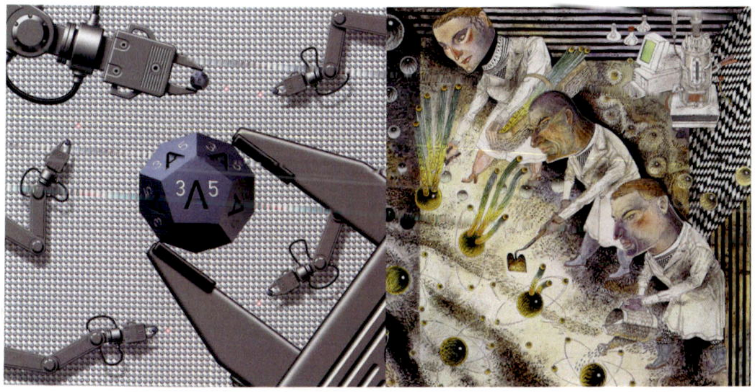

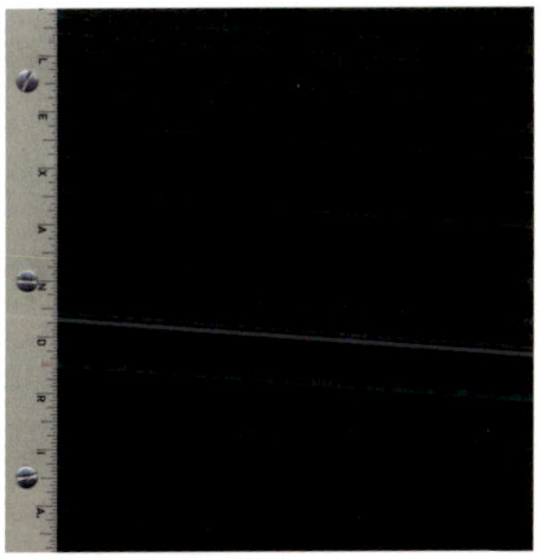

Alexandria Real Estate Equities, Inc.

FIRM_ opto design
ART DIRECTORS_ john klotnia, brad simon
DESIGNERS_ kelly alkins, jennifer wenzlaff
ILLUSTRATORS_ jack unruh, roger spears, neil armstrong, david wilcox, peter kramer, tavis coburn, nick fasciano
PHOTOGRAPHERS_ eric staudenmaier, john paul endress
PRINTER_ colorgraphics

FIRM_ Meta 4 Design, Inc.
ART DIRECTOR_ Fred Biliter
DESIGNER_ Fred Biliter
PHOTOGRAPHERS_ Mark Battrell, Arthur Meyerson
ILLUSTRATOR_ Jerome Lenz
COPYWRITERS_ Ed Kittrell, Chuck Kaiser, Leonard Rau
PRINTER_ Quebecor World-Acme Printing

Allstate

COVER PAPER self cover
TEXT PAPER 80lb. Mohawk cream white vellum cover
COLORS 6
PAGES 8
QUANTITY 426,000

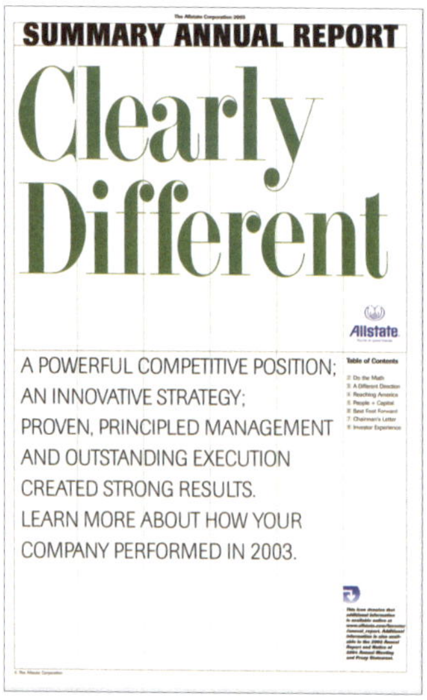

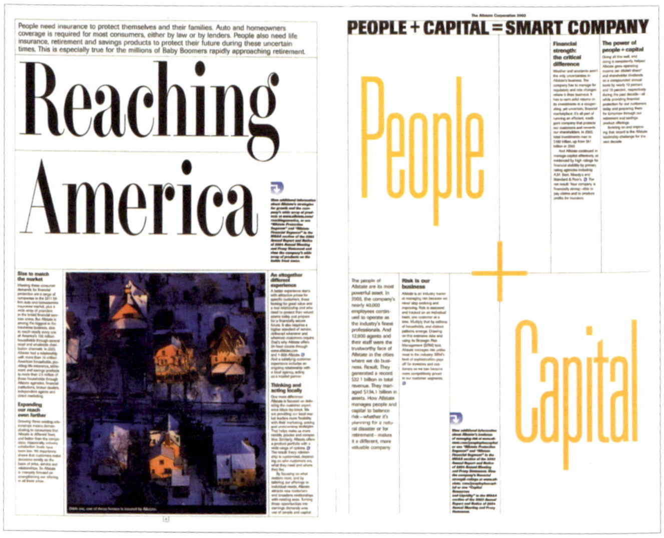

COVER PAPER 100lb. Weyerhaeuser cougar opaque cover
TEXT PAPER 100lb. Weyerhaeuser cougar opaque text
COLORS 6
PAGES 64
QUANTITY 5,000

Altalink

FIRM_ Result Inc.
ART DIRECTOR_ Monique Gamache
DESIGNER_ Monique Gamache
PHOTOGRAPHER_ Chad Johnston
PRINTER_ Sundog Printing

FIRM_ stoyan Design
ART DIRECTORS_ David stoyan wooters, chi Hang
DESIGNER_ chi Hang
PRINTER_ colorGraphics

American Vanguard

COVER PAPER 100lb. Mohawk Navajo
TEXT PAPER 80lb. Mohawk Navajo
COLORS 8
PAGES 62
QUANTITY 8,000

COVER PAPER 100lb. Stora Enso Centura Dull
TEXT PAPERS 100lb. Stora Enso Centura Dull, 80lb. Carnival Vellum Stellar White
COLORS 8
PAGES 72
QUANTITY 18,000

AMB Property Corporation

FIRM_ Eleven Inc.
ART DIRECTOR_ Ted Bluey
DESIGNER_ Ted Bluey
PHOTOGRAPHERS_ Phil Toledano, Doug Gogelson, Alain Giraud
COPYWRITERS_ Bob Price, Lauren Barr
PRINTER_ Anderson Lithograph

FIRM_	SamataMason
ART DIRECTORS_	Kevin Krueger, Greg Samata, Pat Samata
DESIGNERS_	Kevin Krueger, Greg Samata, Pat Samata
PHOTOGRAPHERS_	Dennis Ayuson, Chris Kirzeder, Stock
COPYWRITERS_	AptarGroup, SamataMason
PRINTER_	Blanchette Press

COVER PAPER	110lb. Fraser Papers Pegasus smooth cover
TEXT PAPERS	100lb. Fraser Papers Pegasus smooth Text, 70lb. Fraser Papers Synergy Text
COLORS	6
PAGES	90
QUANTITY	12,000

AptarGroup

COVER PAPER	80lb. Fraser Pegasus Black cover
TEXT PAPERS	80lb. smooth Text Fraser Pegasus Museum white, 100lb. Domtar Luna Gloss white
COLORS	6
PAGES	82
QUANTITY	3,000

Arcis Corporation

FIRM_	SasgesWright Inc.
ART DIRECTOR_	Rita Sasges
DESIGNERS_	Rita Sasges, Isabel Abdai
PHOTOGRAPHERS_	Gerrard Yunker, Phillip Dykes
COPYWRITER_	National PR
PRINTER_	Blanchette Press

FIRM_	addison
ART DIRECTOR_	richard colbourne
DESIGNER_	eunice woo
PHOTOGRAPHER_	michael prince
COPYWRITER_	steve goldstein
PRINTER_	anderson lithograph

Avery Dennison

COVER PAPERS	80lb. Fox River Max opaque vellum cover and text
TEXT PAPERS	80lb. Fox River vellum text, 70lb. Fox River vellum text
COLORS	6
PAGES	78
QUANTITY	97,000

COVER PAPER	80lb. Mohawk options 100% PC white
TEXT PAPER	80lb. Mohawk options 100% PC white
COLORS	8
PAGES	120
QUANTITY	126,000

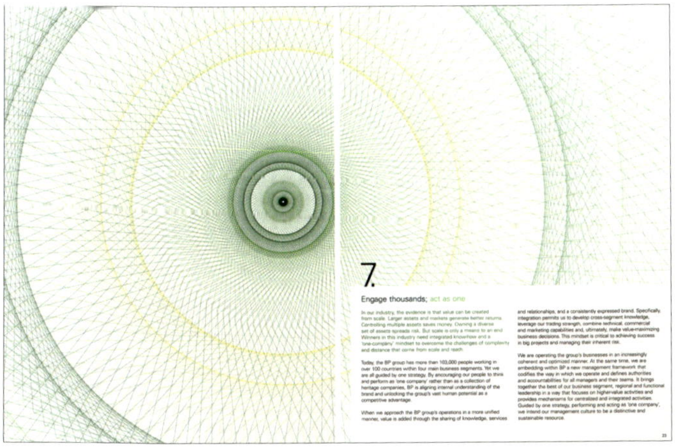

BP

FIRM_	VSA partners
ART DIRECTORS_	Dana Arnett, Jamie Koval
DESIGNERS_	Dan Knuckey, Brock Conrad
PHOTOGRAPHERS_	various
COPYWRITER_	Andy Blankenburg
PRINTERS_	Sandy Alexander, St. Ives Burrups

FIRM_ cahan & associates
ART DIRECTORS_ bill cahan, craig williamson
DESIGNER_ craig williamson
PHOTOGRAPHER_ elena dorfman
COPYWRITERS_ tom mierzwinski, cahan & associates
PRINTER_ colorgraphics

BRE

COVER PAPER 80lb. utopia 2 text
TEXT PAPER 80lb. utopia 2 text
COLORS 6
PAGES 28

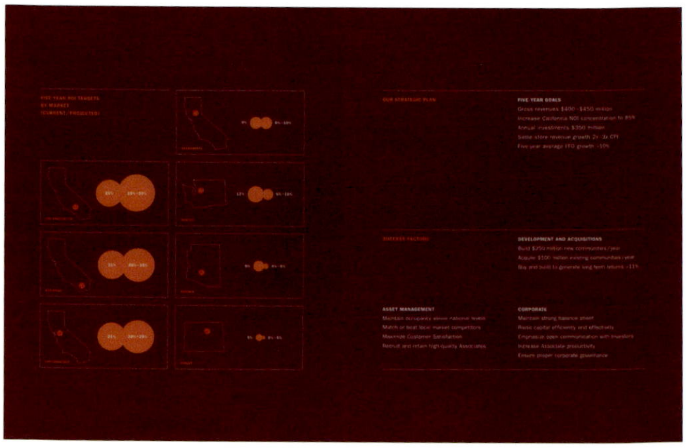

COVER PAPER 93lb. scheufelen north america phoenixmotion xenon cover
TEXT PAPER 90lb. scheufelen north america phoenixmotion xenon text
COLORS 6
PAGES 96
QUANTITY 70,000

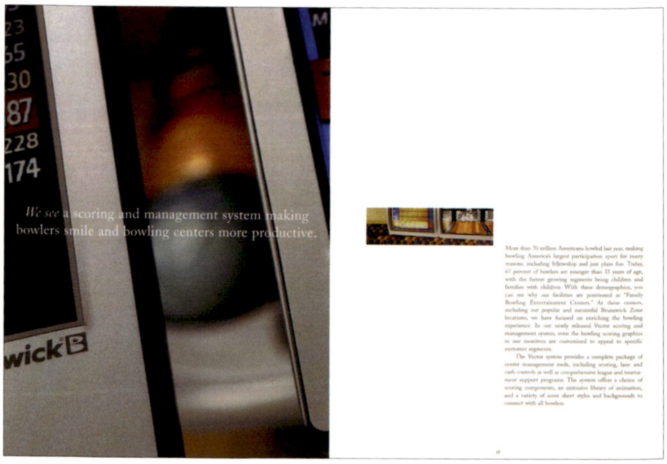

Brunswick Corporation

FIRM_ BHI
ART DIRECTORS_ kerry lacoste, dave lambertsen
DESIGNER_ kerry lacoste
PHOTOGRAPHERS_ joe pellegrini, tony armour
COPYWRITER_ dan kubera/BHI
PRINTER_ lake county press, inc.

FIRM_ methodologie
ART DIRECTORS_ Janet DeDonato, Dale Hart
DESIGNER_ Royal Stuart
PHOTOGRAPHER_ Eric Myer
COPYWRITER_ Hugh Saffel
PRINTER_ Williamson Printing

Burlington Northern Santa Fe

COVER PAPER weyerhauser cougar opaque cover
TEXT PAPER weyerhauser cougar opaque text
COLORS 6
PAGES 90
QUANTITY 150,000

COVER PAPER 80lb. Fox River crushed leaf
TEXT PAPER 100lb. Finch Fine
COLORS 5
PAGES 24
QUANTITY 35,000

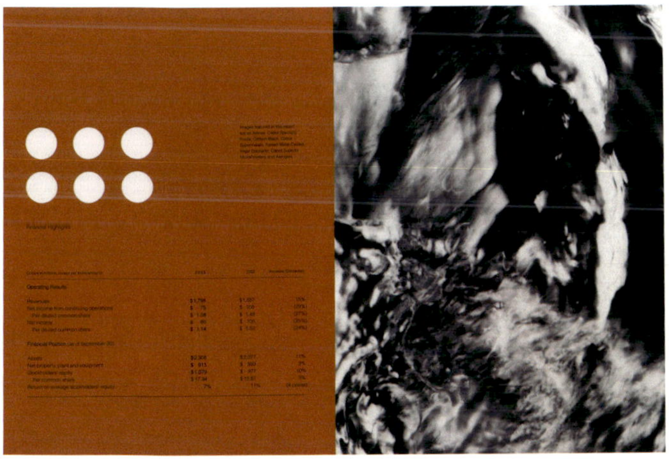

Cabot Corporation

FIRM_ SVP Partners
ART DIRECTORS_ Jean Page, Randy Smith, Bob Vitale
DESIGNERS_ Jean Page, Randy Smith, Bob Vitale
PHOTOGRAPHER_ Jim Coon
COPYWRITER_ Susan Urbanetti
PRINTER_ Merril Daniels

FIRM_ McNulty & Company
ART DIRECTORS_ Dan McNulty, Richard Huvard
DESIGNERS_ Dan McNulty, Ryan Plantin
PHOTOGRAPHER_ Chris Zsarnay
COPYWRITERS_ Richard Huvard, Gerry Freisleben
PRINTER_ Southern California Graphics

COVER PAPER 100lb. Sappi Paper McCoy Silk Book
TEXT PAPER 100lb. Sappi Paper McCoy Silk Book
COLORS 6
PAGES 58
QUANTITY 4,000

Calavo Growers Inc.

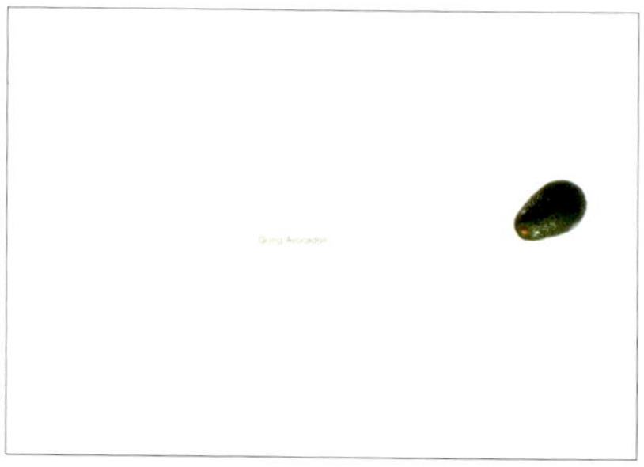

COVER PAPER 80lb. Cougar Opaque Text
TEXT PAPERS 60lb. Fraser Torchglow, 50lb. Offset
COLORS 1
PAGES 12
QUANTITY 2,500

AGRICULTURE

The Calgary Exhibition & Stampede remains a steadfast partner to Alberta's agriculture community in celebrating and supporting that industry's remarkable and enduring economic and cultural contribution. The Calgary Exhibition & Stampede featured a vast menu of agriculture programming throughout 2003 as part of our commitment to create an environment that inspires people to think, promote and sell agriculture. Our diverse activities ranged from the Family Farm Awards to cowboy poetry presentations, from stock dog events to the Seed Fair and Hay Show. The Beef Cattle Program, for example, enhances the value of purebred cattle through presentation and marketing, and in 2003 more than 500 animals were showcased at our cattle shows. We also hosted many educational programs, such as Roughstock 2003, which attracted more than 56,000 visitors from across southern Alberta. This annual spring Western festival brought the country into the city with a mix of education and entertainment, such as Rodeo Royal, one of Canada's premier rodeos, and the Blackstar Saloon. The four-day festival featured several other key programs. Aggie Days introduced over 7,000 elementary students and teachers to the agriculture industry in 2003. Created in conjunction with major agricultural partners, this fun, interactive program was presented by volunteers from 13 committees, industry representatives and producers. Family Fun Days was a free celebration of agriculture and farm life. It included interactive displays and forums for industry experts to provide information on produce, nutrition and food safety. More than 25,000 people attended Family Fun Days in 2003, and the overall program saw an increase of 10 per cent from the previous year. The Acreage Lifestyle Show was a popular consumer show catering to the acreage owner, hobby farmers and others who enjoy the rural lifestyle. The show featured business and service exhibits as well as information seminars. We also helped link agriculture to Calgary's arts community in some innovative ways last July. The Agrium Heavy Horse Show and the Calgary Philharmonic Orchestra teamed up to entertain over 30,000 people with an equine symphony. Forty musicians accompanied the powerful rhythm stamped out by teams of heavy horses competing for the World Six-Horse Hitch Championship. In addition, we showcased the first Metal Art Showcase as a celebration of blacksmithing artistry. Metal artworks entered in the Creative Forging class at the World Championship Blacksmith Competition were put on display at an elegant wine and cheese reception, where art lovers met the artists and bid on their works in exciting live and silent auctions. A new partnership between the Stampede, the International Stockmen's Education Foundation and the Canadian Cattlemen Association brought 250 beef industry leaders from around the world to Stampede Park in July. The first annual International Beef Industry Congress explored challenges and opportunities facing the industry and was an important forum for fostering industry cooperation across borders. In May at the 4-H on Parade, one of the largest shows of its kind in North America, more than 800 young people celebrated the 90th anniversary of 4-H in Canada. Hosted by the Calgary Stampede and organized by a volunteer committee, the 2003 program was a nostalgic look at agriculture's roots and an inspiring glimpse into the future. The Stampede is proud to present a wide range of 4-H programs that educate, motivate and empower southern Alberta youth. The Junior Livestock Evaluation Seminar in December gave young stock enthusiasts a full day to practice real-world skills they'll need to become future leaders in the livestock industry. Instructors from the livestock community volunteered their time, sharing their expertise with a new generation of farmers and ranchers. Because neighbours help neighbours when times are tough, in 2003 the Stampede organized and hosted a Unity Barbeque in conjunction with the City of Calgary's simulcast of the SARS Relief Concert from Toronto. More than 8,000 Calgarians enjoyed live entertainment, savoured a free Alberta beef barbeque provided by The Ranchmans Renegades, and donated $5,000 to the Alberta Beef Producers (ABP). Stampede facilities were again the site of an Olds College satellite campus in 2003, offering traditional training in agriculture and equine activities, as well as courses in gardening, land management and composting.

Calgary Exhibition & Stampede

FIRM_ Highwood Communications Ltd.
ART DIRECTORS_ Steve Williams, Keli Pollock, Monique Gamache
DESIGNER_ Monique Gamache
PHOTOGRAPHER_ Jared Sych
COPYWRITERS_ Nancy Cope, Lindsey Galloway
PRINTERS_ Calgary Colorpress, Sundog Printing

FIRM_ campbell sheffield design
ART DIRECTOR_ paul campbell
DESIGNER_ Lisa Di Minno
PHOTOGRAPHER_ andrew easson
COPYWRITER_ Todd Minerson
PRINTER_ somerset graphics co. ltd.

Casey House Foundation

COVER PAPER 100lb. productolith matte cover
TEXT PAPER 100lb. productolith matte text
COLORS 5
PAGES 36
QUANTITY 2,500

COVER PAPER 100lb. Monadock Astrolite white cover
TEXT PAPERS 100lb. Monadock white text, 80lb. Nexfor Fraser synergy citrus text
COLORS 8
PAGES 48
QUANTITY 15,000

CEC Entertainment

FIRM_ squires + company
ART DIRECTOR_ Brandon Murphy
DESIGNER_ Adam Hallmark
PHOTOGRAPHER_ Andy Bennett
COPYWRITER_ Laurie Hesser
PRINTER_ padgett printing

FIRM_ Leonhardt:Fitch
ART DIRECTOR_ Marcela Barrientos
DESIGNER_ Marcela Barrientos
PHOTOGRAPHER_ Young Lee
COPYWRITER_ Devin Liddell
PRINTER_ Colorgraphics

Cell Therapeutics, Inc.

COVER PAPER 100lb. Sappi McCoy Matte Cover
TEXT PAPER 100lb. Sappi McCoy Matte Text
COLORS 8
PAGES 28
QUANTITY 20,000

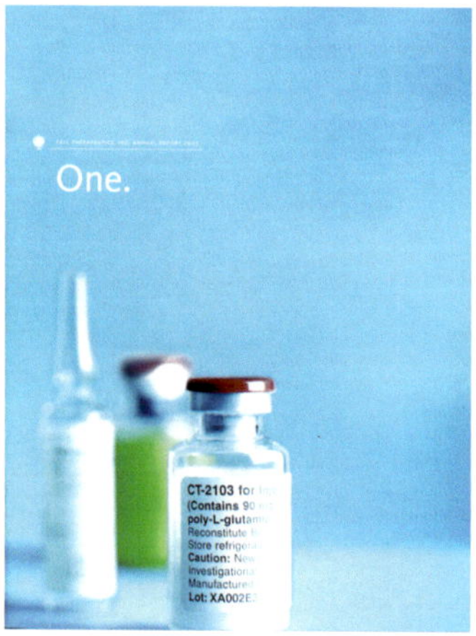

COVER PAPER Centura Matte
TEXT PAPER Centura Matte
COLORS 4
PAGES 96
QUANTITY 160,000

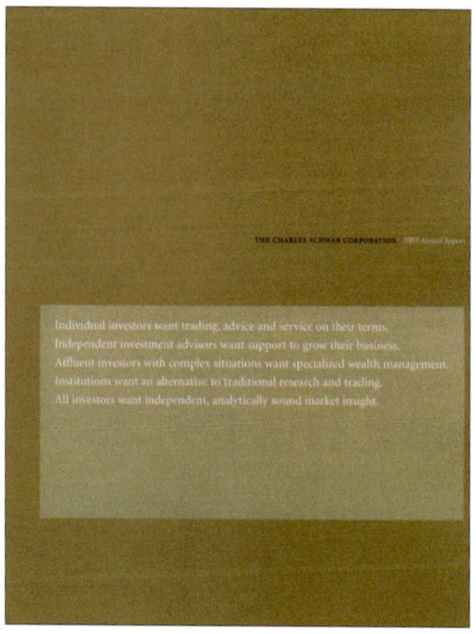

Charles Schwab

FIRM_ Cahan & Associates
ART DIRECTORS_ Bill Cahan, Kevin Roberson
DESIGNER_ Kevin Roberson
COPYWRITER_ Tim Peters
PRINTER_ Lithographix

FIRM_	sequel studio
ART DIRECTOR_	Bret Gerstenblatt
DESIGNER_	Bazil Findlay
PHOTOGRAPHER_	craig cutler
COPYWRITER_	Margot Witty
PRINTER_	sandy alexander

Chelsea Property Group

COVER PAPER	80lb. carnival cover
TEXT PAPER	100lb. carnival text
COLORS	8
PAGES	74
QUANTITY	25,500

COLORS	2
PAGES	96
QUANTITY	5,000

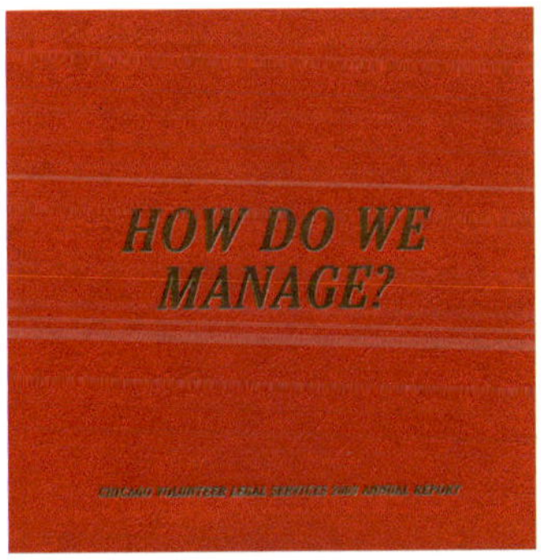

Chicago Volunteer Legal Services

FIRM_	Lowercase, Inc.
ART DIRECTOR_	Tim Bruce
DESIGNER_	Tim Bruce
PHOTOGRAPHER_	Tony Armour
PRINTER_	Blanchette Press

FIRM_ samatamason
ART DIRECTOR_ Greg Samata
DESIGNER_ Beth May
PHOTOGRAPHERS_ Chris Kirzeder, stock
COPYWRITER_ Betty Brisk
PRINTER_ Blanchette Press

Children's Home and Aid Society

COVER PAPER 100lb. sappi mccoy matte cover
TEXT PAPER 80lb. sappi mccoy matte text
COLORS 5
PAGES 44
QUANTITY 4,000

COVER PAPER 100lb. mohawk superfine ultrawhite eggshell cover
TEXT PAPERS 60lb. mohawk superfine ultrawhite smooth cover, 70lb. mohawk options warmwhite text
COLORS 7
PAGES 76
QUANTITY 10,000

Coca-Cola Femsa

FIRM_ Paragraphs Design
ART DIRECTORS_ Meow Vatanatumrak, Rachel Radtke, Robin Zvonek
DESIGNER_ Meow Vatanatumrak
PHOTOGRAPHER_ Gabriel Covian
ILLUSTRATORS_ Peter Horjus, Fernando Andriacci
COPYWRITER_ Peter Warrick
PRINTER_ Quantum Color Graphics

FIRM_	Turner & Associates
ART DIRECTOR_	Steve Turner
DESIGNER_	Laura Milton
PHOTOGRAPHERS_	Angie Wyant, Jock McDonald
COPYWRITER_	Terry London
PRINTER_	Watermark Press

Cost Plus World Market

COVER PAPER	80lb. Fox River Confetti
TEXT PAPER	65lb. Mohawk Options
COLORS	5
PAGES	51
QUANTITY	11,000

COVER PAPER	.088 board casebound Black Pearl Linen
TEXT PAPERS	100lb. Sappi McCoy Matte Text, 80lb. Mohawk Warm White Vellum Text
COLORS	8
PAGES	86
QUANTITY	13,000

Courier Corporation

FIRM_	Weymouth Design
ART DIRECTOR_	Robert Krivicich
DESIGNER_	Aaron Haesaert
PHOTOGRAPHER_	Michael Weymouth
COPYWRITER_	John Temple
PRINTER_	Quebecor World Acme

FIRM_ Douglas Joseph Partners
ART DIRECTORS_ Doug Joseph, Scott Lambert
DESIGNER_ Scott Lambert
ILLUSTRATORS_ Carol Fabricatore; calligrapher: Elli Evertsen
COPYWRITER_ Larry Pearson
PRINTER_ Anderson Lithograph

COVER PAPER 110lb. Nexfor Fraser Pegasus Brilliant White Super Smooth Cover
TEXT PAPERS 100lb. Sappi McCoy Uncoated Text, 100lb. Nexfor Fraser Papers Pegasus Brilliant White Vellum Text
COLORS 8
PAGES 50
QUANTITY 10,000

Entravision Communications

COVER PAPER 100lb. Mead Westvaco Sterling White Cover
TEXT PAPER 100lb. Mead Westvaco Sterling White Text
COLORS 10
PAGES 90
QUANTITY 28,000

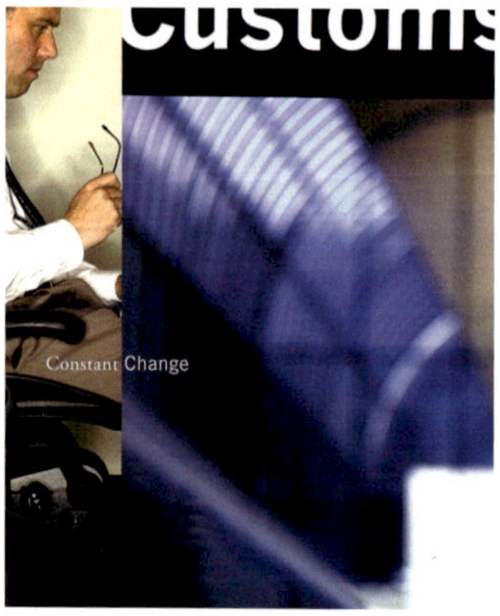

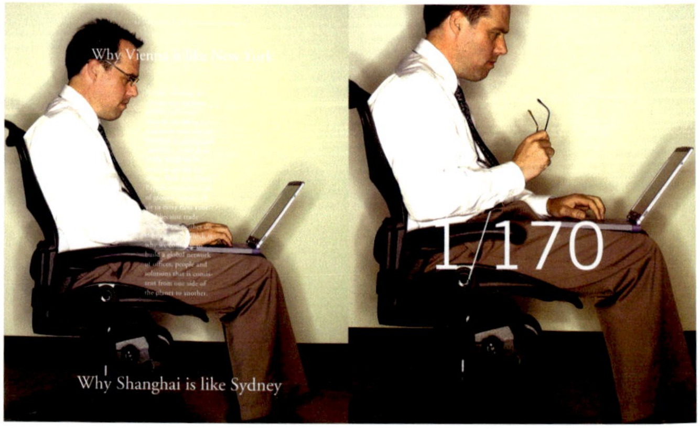

Expeditors International of Washington, Inc.

FIRM_ Leimer Cross Design
ART DIRECTOR_ Kerry Leimer
DESIGNER_ Kerry Leimer
PHOTOGRAPHER_ Eric Myer
COPYWRITER_ Kerry Leimer
PRINTER_ Blanchette Press

FIRM_ EAI
ART DIRECTOR_ David Cannon
DESIGNER_ Nicole Riekki
PHOTOGRAPHERS_ Derek Shapton, Christopher Wahl
COPYWRITER_ Frank Oswald
PRINTER_ Lithographix

FedEx

COVER PAPER	80lb. Mohawk Options True White Smooth Cover
TEXT PAPERS	80lb. Mohawk Options True White Smooth Text, 60lb. International Paper via Bright White Smooth Text
COLORS	6
PAGES	80
QUANTITY	275,000

COVER PAPER	80lb. Mohawk Options Warm White Smooth Cover
TEXT PAPERS	80lb. Mohawk Satin Warm White Smooth Text, 60lb. Mohawk Satin Warm White Smooth Text
COLORS	7
PAGES	92
QUANTITY	300,000

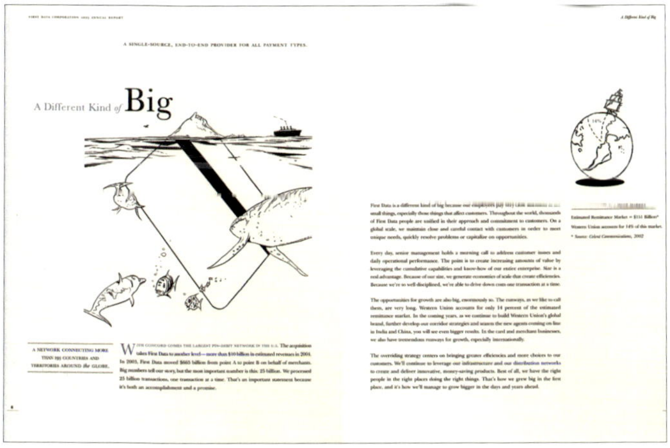

First Data Corporation

FIRM_ VSA Partners
ART DIRECTORS_ Dana Arnett, Steve Ryan
DESIGNERS_ Steve Ryan, Luke Galambos
ILLUSTRATOR_ Istvan Banyai
COPYWRITER_ Mike Noble
PRINTER_ Hennegan

FIRM_	Petrick Design
ART DIRECTOR_	Robert Petrick
DESIGNER_	Tracy West
ILLUSTRATOR_	Brenda Brown
COPYWRITER_	Bruce Hetrick
PRINTER_	Lake County Press

COVER PAPERS 80lb. Fibermark, Leatherette jersey cover
TEXT PAPERS 70lb. Domtar Whitehall smooth text, 80lb. Scheufelen North America, Inc. Gleneagle gloss text
COLORS 3
PAGES 152
QUANTITY 33,150

First Health

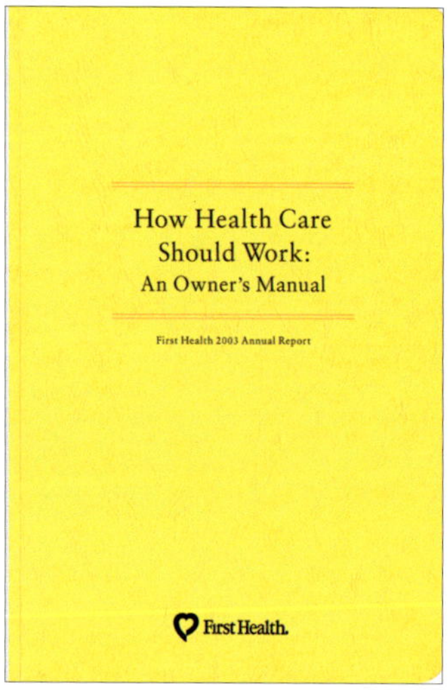

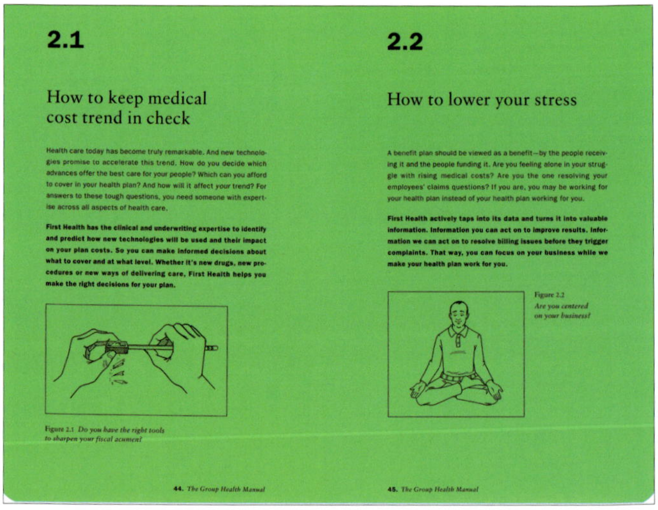

COVER PAPER 100lb. Unisource Corniche velvet cover
TEXT PAPERS 100lb. Corniche velvet text, 70lb. Bradner Smith & Company High Impact opaque text
COLORS 5
PAGES 68
QUANTITY 40,000

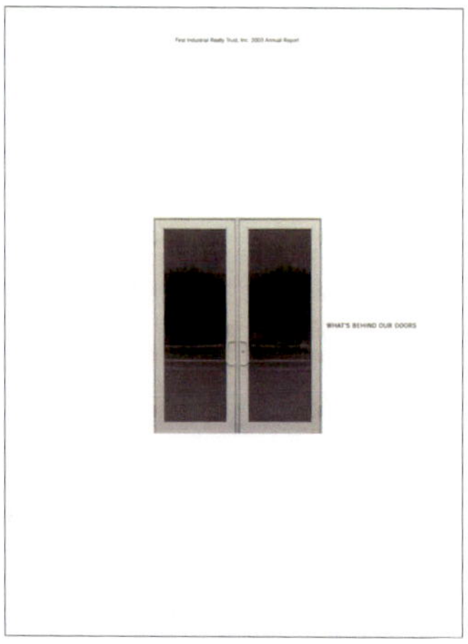

First Industrial Realty Trust, Inc.

FIRM_	BHI
ART DIRECTORS_	Kerry Lacoste, Dave Lambertsen
DESIGNER_	Audrey Roberts
PHOTOGRAPHER_	Charlie Westerman
COPYWRITER_	Mike Daly/BHI
PRINTER_	Consolidated Carqueville Printing Co.

FIRM_ squires & company
ART DIRECTOR_ Brandon Murphy
DESIGNER_ Brandon Murphy
PHOTOGRAPHERS_ Andy Bennett, Scott Metcalfe
COPYWRITER_ Max Wright
PRINTER_ Williamson Printing

First State Bancorporation

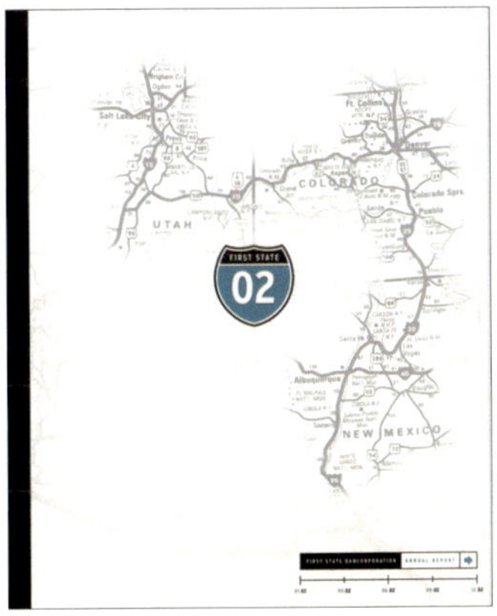

COVER PAPER 100lb. Fox River Coranado Smooth White Cover
TEXT PAPERS 100lb. Fox River Coranado White Text,
70lb. Sundance Smoke Text
COLORS 6
PAGES 84
QUANTITY 7,000

COVER PAPER 100lb. Finch Fine Basis Bright White Fine Cover
TEXT PAPERS 100lb. Finch Fine Basis Bright White Fine Text,
80lb. International Paper Vellum Ivory Text
COLORS 4
PAGES 60
QUANTITY 6,000

The Fresh Air Fund

FIRM_ Suka Design
ART DIRECTOR_ Brian Wong
DESIGNER_ Brian Wong
PRINTERS_ Andrew Connecticut
RR Donnelley Co.

FIRM_ addison
ART DIRECTOR_ david kohler
DESIGNER_ john moon
PHOTOGRAPHERS_ todd goebel, charlie westerman
COPYWRITER_ rhonda johnson
PRINTER_ digital color concepts

COVER PAPER 80lb. mohawk superfine white smooth
TEXT PAPERS 100lb. mohawk superfine white smooth, 50lb. cream vellum
COLORS 7
PAGES 112
QUANTITY 33,000

GATX

TEXT PAPERS 60lb. weyerhaeuser cougar opaque smooth text, 50lb. cougar opaque smooth text
COLORS 5
PAGES 68
QUANTITY 10,000

Gay Men's Health Crisis

FIRM_ baileyco.-NYC
ART DIRECTOR_ craig bailey
DESIGNER_ craig bailey
PHOTOGRAPHER_ john arsenault
COPYWRITER_ matthew montelongo
PRINTER_ JCI graphics

FIRM_ Nesnadny + Schwartz, Cleveland + New York + Toronto
ART DIRECTOR_ Mark Schwartz
DESIGNERS_ Michelle Moehler, Joyce Nesnadny
PHOTOGRAPHER_ Andrew Borowiec
COPYWRITERS_ Geoffrey Gund, David Abbott, Deena Epstein
PRINTER_ Fortran Printing

The George Gund Foundation

COVER PAPER 140lb. French Muscletone Black Cover
TEXT PAPERS 100lb. Appleton Utopia One X Xtra Bright Silk Text, 60lb. French Durotone Primer Gold Text, 80lb. French Durotone Packing Box Board Text
COLORS 5
PAGES 50
QUANTITY 3,500

COVER PAPER 80lb. M-Real Galerie Art Silk Cover
TEXT PAPER 80lb. M-Real Galerie Art Silk Cover
COLORS 4
PAGES 30
QUANTITY 2,200

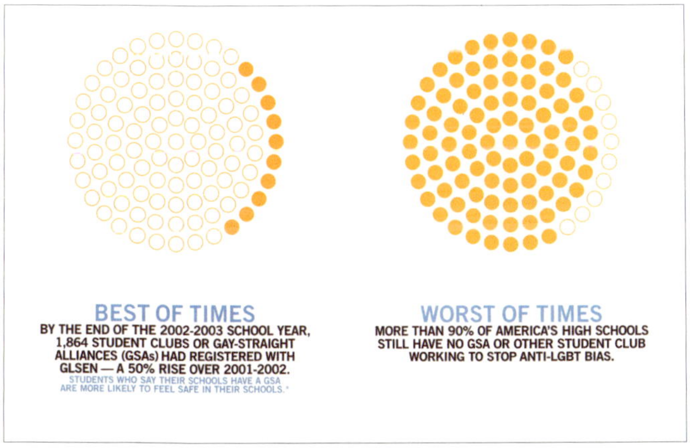

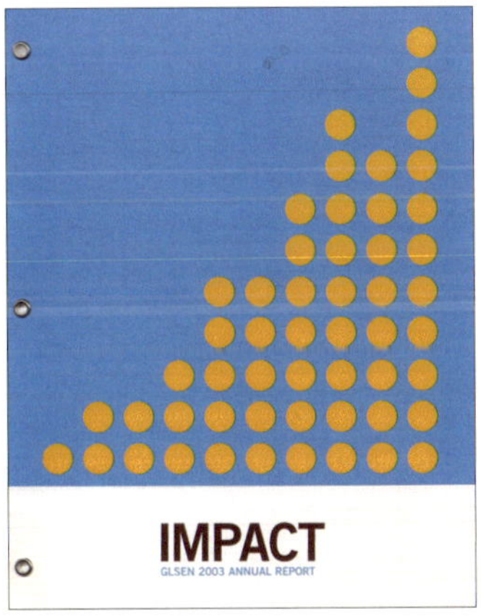

GLSEN

FIRM_ Suka Design
ART DIRECTOR_ Brian Wong
DESIGNER_ Brian Wong
ILLUSTRATOR_ Brian Wong
PRINTER_ Conceptual Litho Reproductions

FIRM_ cahan & associates
ART DIRECTORS_ bill cahan, michael braley
DESIGNER_ michael braley
PHOTOGRAPHER_ jock mcdonald
COPYWRITER_ thom elkjer
PRINTER_ anderson lithograph

Greater Bay Bancorp

COVER PAPER 65lb. cougar opaque cover
TEXT PAPER 80lb. mccoy silk text
COLORS 6
PAGES 44
QUANTITY 30,000

COVER PAPER 100lb. fox river paper starwhite tiara vellum text
TEXT PAPER 100lb. fox river paper starwhite tiara vellum text
COLORS 4
PAGES 44
QUANTITY 2,000

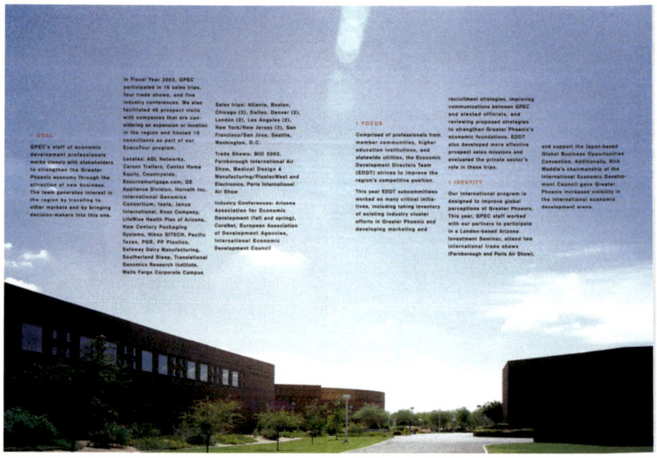

Greater Phoenix Economic Council

FIRM_ fervor creative
ART DIRECTORS_ don newlen, jami pomponi alire
DESIGNER_ paul reed
PHOTOGRAPHERS_ paul reed, don newlen, wayne rainey
COPYWRITER_ krissy miskovsky
PRINTER_ o'neil printing

FIRM_	VSA Partners
ART DIRECTOR_	Jason Jones
DESIGNER_	Jacob Gardner
PHOTOGRAPHER_	Charlie Simokaitis
COPYWRITERS_	Bob Klein, Harley-Davidson
PRINTER_	Litho, Inc.

Harley–Davidson

COVER PAPER	80lb. Fox River Sundance Ultra White Smooth Cover
TEXT PAPER	80lb. Fox River Sundance Ultra White Smooth Text
COLORS	6
PAGES	98
QUANTITY	425,000

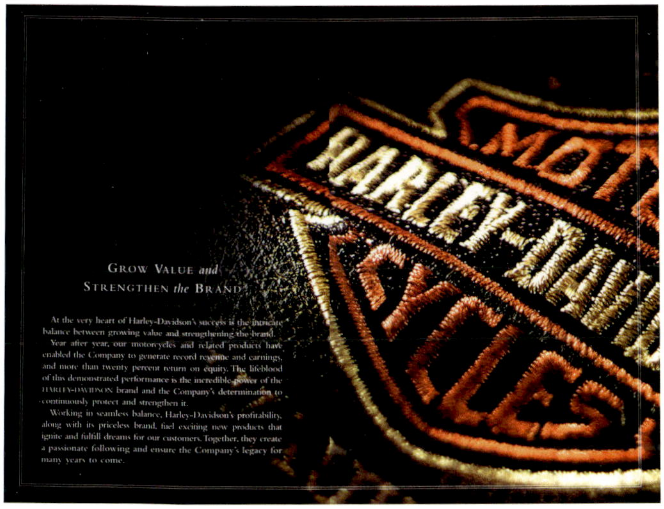

COVER PAPER	80lb. Mohawk Options
TEXT PAPER	100lb. Mohawk Options
COLORS	2
PAGES	20
QUANTITY	2,000

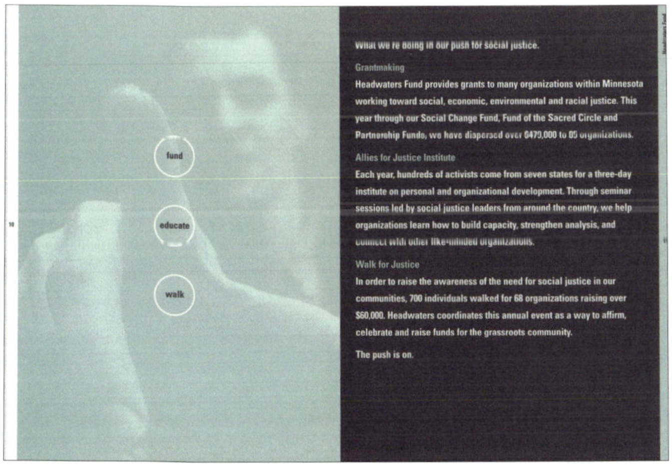

Headwaters Fund

FIRM_	ThinkDesign Group
ART DIRECTOR_	Linda Henneman
DESIGNER_	Linda Henneman
PHOTOGRAPHER_	Stock
COPYWRITER_	Jonathan Wiese
PRINTER_	Bruce Printing

Herman Miller, Inc.

COVER PAPER 65lb. wausau exact opaque smooth white cover
TEXT PAPERS 70lb. wausau exact opaque smooth white text, 80lb. exact opaque smooth white text
COLORS 5
PAGES 50
QUANTITY 22,000

FIRM_ Herman Miller
ART DIRECTOR_ stephen frykholm
DESIGNERS_ stephen frykhom, andrew dull
PHOTOGRAPHERS_ james warych, bill sharpe, nick merrick, fracois robert, william hebert
COPYWRITER_ clark malcolm
PRINTER_ steketee-van huis, inc.

IBM (2002)

COVER PAPER 80lb. mohawk options true white vellum cover
TEXT PAPER 80lb. mohawk options true white vellum text
COLORS 8
PAGES 76
QUANTITY 60,000

FIRM_ VSA
ART DIRECTORS_ curt schreiber, ashley lippard
DESIGNER_ claudia alberts
PHOTOGRAPHER_ charlie simokaitis
COPYWRITER_ IBM
PRINTER_ anderson lithograph

FIRM_ vsa partners
ART DIRECTOR_ curt schreiber
DESIGNERS_ ashley lippard, greg sylvester, michelle platts
PHOTOGRAPHERS_ christian witkin, dan winters, carlos serrao, julian broad
PRINTER_ anderson lithograph

IBM (2003)

- COVER PAPER 80lb. mohawk options true white vellum cover
- TEXT PAPERS 70lb. mead sterling ultra white gloss text, 50lb. opaque vellum text
- COLORS 8
- PAGES 128
- QUANTITY 2,500,000

- COVER PAPER 90lb. mohawk
- TEXT PAPER 100lb. mohawk
- COLORS 8
- PAGES 26
- QUANTITY 60 million

IMS Health Inc.

FIRM_ sequel studio
ART DIRECTOR_ brett gerstenslatt
DESIGNER_ bazil findlay
PHOTOGRAPHER_ michael prince
COPYWRITER_ in house
PRINTER_ sandy alexander

FIRM_ Weymouth Design
ART DIRECTOR_ Tom Laidlaw
DESIGNERS_ Arvi Raquel-Santos, Brad Lewthwaite
PHOTOGRAPHER_ Michael Weymouth
COPYWRITER_ Janet Point
PRINTER_ Lithographix, Inc.

COVER PAPER 100lb. Sappi McCoy Silk Cover
TEXT PAPERS 100lb. Sappi McCoy Uncoated Smooth Text, 80lb. Sappi McCoy Uncoated Smooth Text
COLORS 8
PAGES 78
QUANTITY 55,000

InterDigital Communications Corporation

COVER PAPER 80lb. Fraser Papers Pegasus Vellum Cover
TEXT PAPERS 70lb. Fraser Papers Pegasus Vellum Text, 80lb. Domtar Luna Silk Text
COLORS 7
PAGES 64
QUANTITY 25,000

Intrawest Corporation

FIRM_ SamataMason
ART DIRECTORS_ Dave Mason, Pamela Lee
DESIGNERS_ Pamela Lee, Keith Leinweber
PHOTOGRAPHERS_ Various
ILLUSTRATOR_ Keith Leinweber
PRINTER_ Blanchette Press

FIRM_	Addison
ART DIRECTOR_	Richard Colbourne
DESIGNER_	Christina Antonopoulos
PHOTOGRAPHERS_	Lorne Bridgman, Vincent Dixon
PRINTER_	Innovation Printing

iStar Financial

COVER PAPER	100lb. Sappi Mccoy matte cover
TEXT PAPERS	100lb. Sappi Mccoy matte text, 80lb. IP Via pure white vellum text
COLORS	7
PAGES	102
QUANTITY	62,500

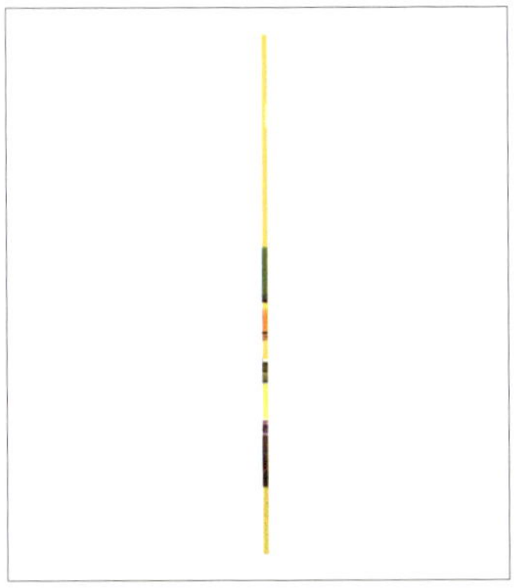

COVER PAPER	100lb. Sappi Mccoy uncoated cover
TEXT PAPER	100lb. Sappi Mccoy matte text
COLORS	8
PAGES	88
QUANTITY	27,000

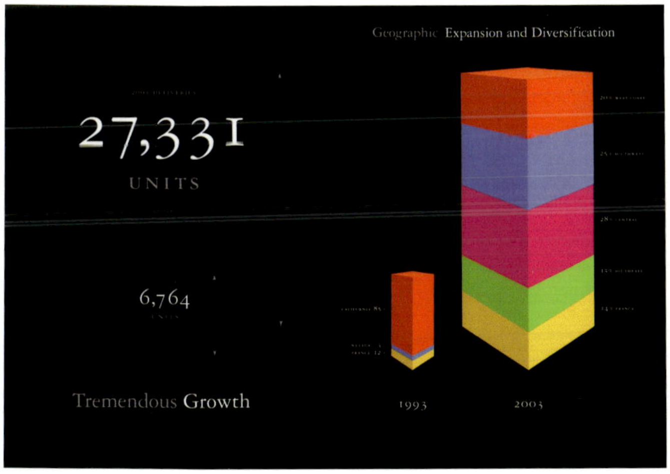

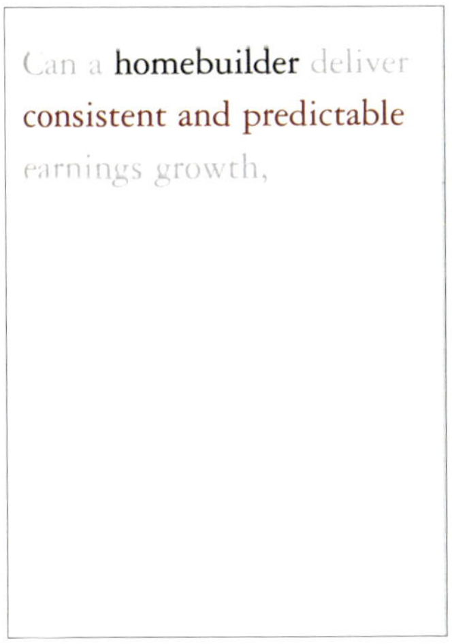

KB Home

FIRM_	Louey/Rubino Design Group Inc.
ART DIRECTOR_	Robert Louey
DESIGNERS_	Robert Louey, Javier Leguizamo
PHOTOGRAPHERS_	Jeff Corwin, Jamey Stillings
ILLUSTRATION_	Javier Leguizamo
COPYWRITER_	David Berger
PRINTER_	Lithographics, Inc.

FIRM_ curran & connors, inc.
ART DIRECTORS_ kim ann piccora; kenneth cole productions, inc.: leslie kolk, chris yoham
PHOTOGRAPHER_ richard avedon studio
COPYWRITERS_ alex dixie, brett minieri
PRINTER_ coral color

Kenneth Cole Productions, Inc.

COVER PAPER sappi mccoy silk
TEXT PAPER sappi mccoy silk
COLORS 6
QUANTITY 7,500

COVER PAPER 100lb. international paper Hammermill via pure white cover
TEXT PAPER 100lb. international paper Hammermill via pure white text
COLORS 5
PAGES 32
QUANTITY 3,000

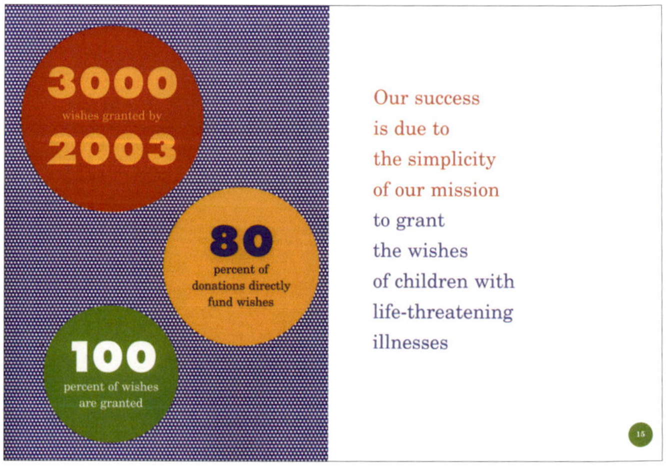

Greater Bay Area Make-A-Wish Foundation

FIRM_ argus
ART DIRECTOR_ jeff breidenbach
DESIGNER_ jeff breidenbach
PHOTOGRAPHER_ theresa vargo
COPYWRITERS_ jeff breidenbach, pat bowers
PRINTER_ oscar printing

FIRM_	SamataMason
ART DIRECTOR_	Greg Samata
DESIGNER_	Beth May
PHOTOGRAPHERS_	Sandro, Dennis Ayuson
COPYWRITERS_	Tracy Shilobrit, Bruce Bock
PRINTER_	Blanchette Press

Manpower, Inc.

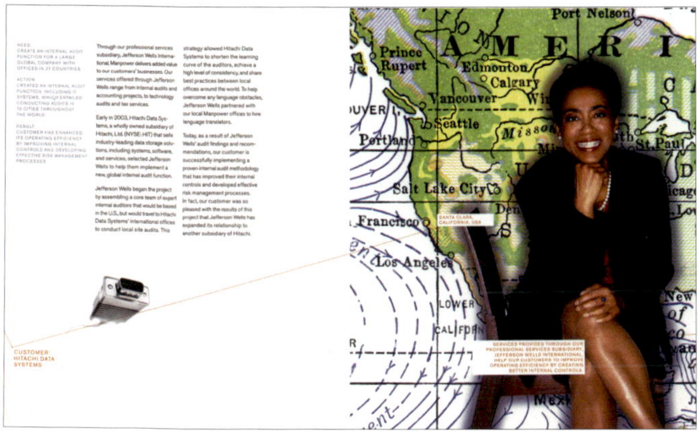

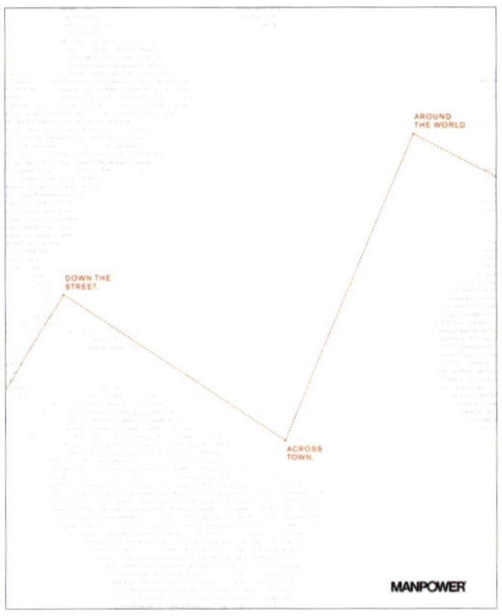

COVER PAPERS	80lb. Sappi Hanno Art Silk Cover
TEXT PAPERS	80lb. Sappi Hanno Art Text French Folded, 80lb. Fraser Papers Pegasus Smooth Text, 60lb. Fraser Papers Glacier Smooth Text
COLORS	6
PAGES	86
QUANTITY	50,000

COVER PAPER	100lb. Finch Fine Vanilla Cover; poster cover wrap on Foster Brights Gold
TEXT PAPER	100lb. Finch Fine Vanilla Text
COLORS	6
PAGES	32
QUANTITY	3,000

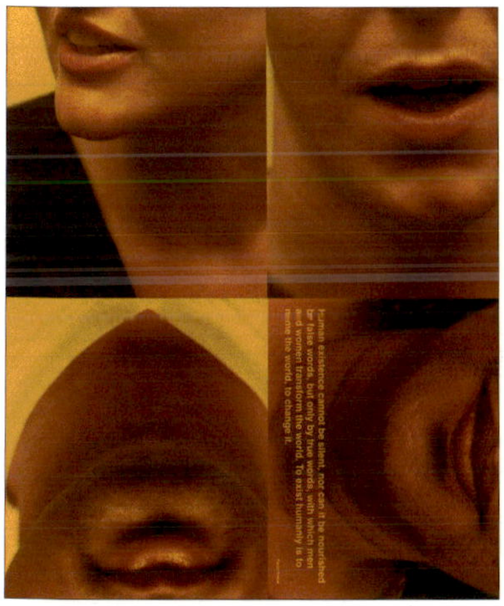

Marguerite Casey Foundation

FIRM_	Methodologie
ART DIRECTOR_	Anne Traver
DESIGNER_	Minh Nguyen
PHOTOGRAPHERS_	Mary Jo McConahay, Young Lee, Kathleen King
COPYWRITERS_	Mary Jo McConahay, David Brotherton
PRINTER_	Colorgraphics

FIRM_	cahan & associates
ART DIRECTORS_	bill cahan, craig williamson
DESIGNER_	craig williamson
COPYWRITER_	alison trollope
PRINTER_	anderson lithograph

COVER PAPER	80lb. utopia 2 blue white matte
TEXT PAPER	80lb. utopia 2 blue white matte
COLORS	8
PAGES	40
QUANTITY	15,000

Maxygen

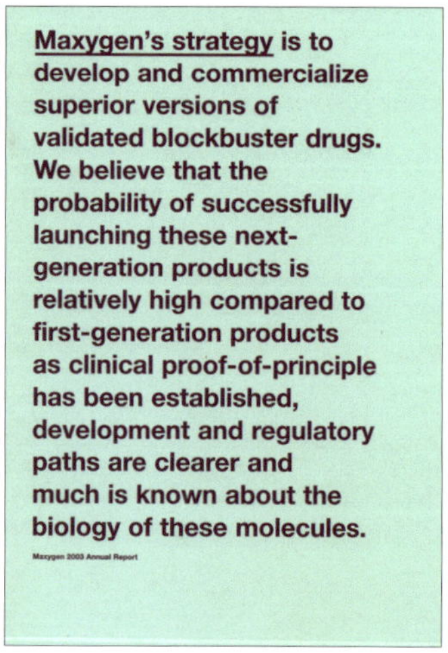

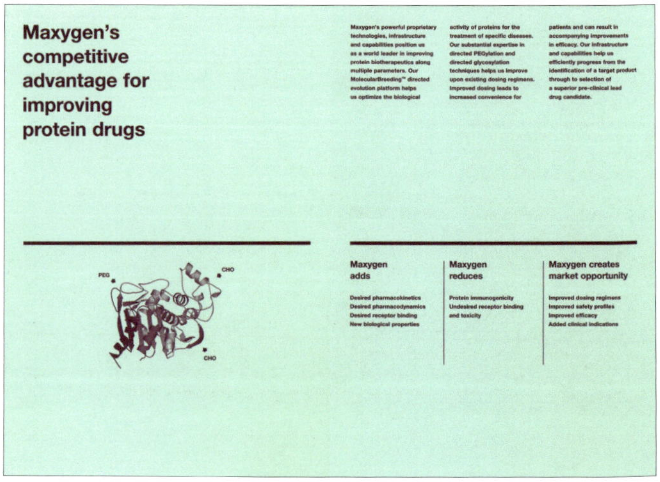

COVER PAPER	100lb. zanders mega dull cover
TEXT PAPERS	100lb. zanders mega dull cover 70lb. finch casblanca opaque vellum
COLORS	7
PAGES	84
QUANTITY	100,000

The McGraw-Hill Companies

FIRM_	addison
ART DIRECTOR_	david kohler
DESIGNER_	craig dobie
PHOTOGRAPHERS_	david katzenstein, brad trent
COPYWRITER_	steven kennedy
PRINTER_	JFB & sons lithographers

FIRM_	McNulty & company
ART DIRECTORS_	eugene bustillos, richard huvard
DESIGNERS_	eugene bustillos, ryan plantin
ILLUSTRATORS_	gavin reece, alexis brandon
COPYWRITER_	richard huvard
PRINTER_	colorgraphics

Mentor Corporation

COVER PAPER	100lb. spicers paper endevour matt cover
TEXT PAPER	100lb. spicers paper endevour text
COLORS	6
PAGES	62
QUANTITY	15,000

COVER PAPER	80lb. mccoy matte cover
TEXT PAPER	100lb. mccoy matte text
COLORS	7
PAGES	ε4
QUANTITY	20,000

Mercury General Corporation

FIRM_	cmg design inc.
ART DIRECTOR_	greg crawford
DESIGNERS_	hollie greenwood, anne marie singer
PHOTOGRAPHER_	greg crawford
COPYWRITER_	david novak
PRINTER_	southern california graphics

MFI

FIRM_	SAS
ART DIRECTORS_	Andy Spencer, Gilmar Wendt, David Stocks
DESIGNERS_	Andy Spencer, Manja Hellpap
PHOTOGRAPHER_	Matt Stuart
COPYWRITER_	Martin Peacock
PRINTER_	Fulmar Colour Printing

COVER PAPER	300GSM GF Smith Zen Pure
TEXT PAPER	150GSM GF Smith Zen Pure
COLORS	5
PAGES	77
QUANTITY	25,000

COVER PAPER	100lb. Mohawk Navajo Text
TEXT PAPER	50lb. Mohawk Navajo Text
COLORS	6
PAGES	12
QUANTITY	3.3 Million

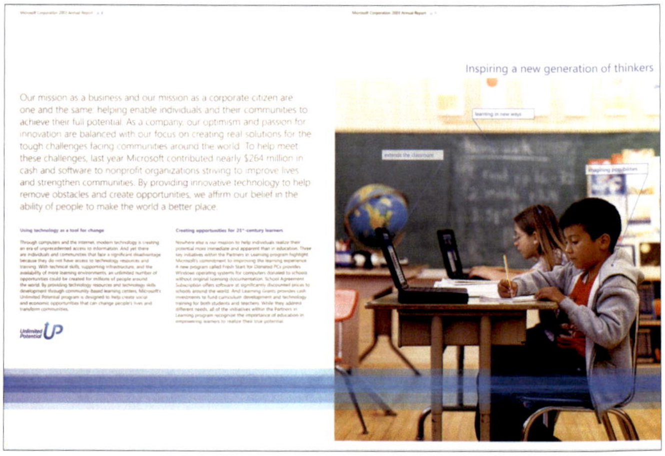

Microsoft Corporation

FIRM_	Leonhardt:Fitch
ART DIRECTORS_	Ray Ueno, Steve Watson
DESIGNERS_	Marcela Barrientos, Ben Graham, Lesley Feldman
PHOTOGRAPHER_	Misha Gravenor
COPYWRITERS_	Devin Liddell, Barry Mitzman
PRINTER_	ColorGraphics

FIRM_ Savage Design Group, Inc.
ART DIRECTOR_ Dahlia Salazar
DESIGNER_ Dahlia Salazar
PHOTOGRAPHERS_ Mark Green, Terry Vine
COPYWRITERS_ Bill Wright, Denny Smith
PRINTER_ Wetmore Printing

Nabors Industries

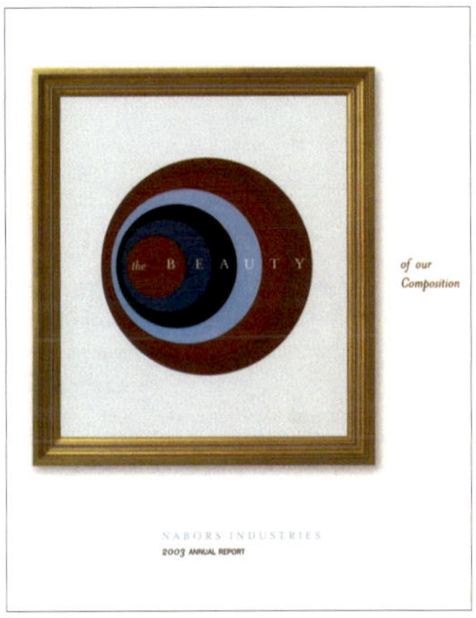

COVER PAPER 130lb. DTC Coronado Infinite white stipple finish
TEXT PAPERS 100lb. Coronado Infinite white stipple finish text, 70lb. Cougar Bright white text
COLORS 10
PAGES 108
QUANTITY 80,000

COVER PAPER 65lb. Utopia 2 white matte cover
TEXT PAPER 70lb. Utopia 2 white matte text
COLORS 8
PAGES 32
QUANTITY 8,500

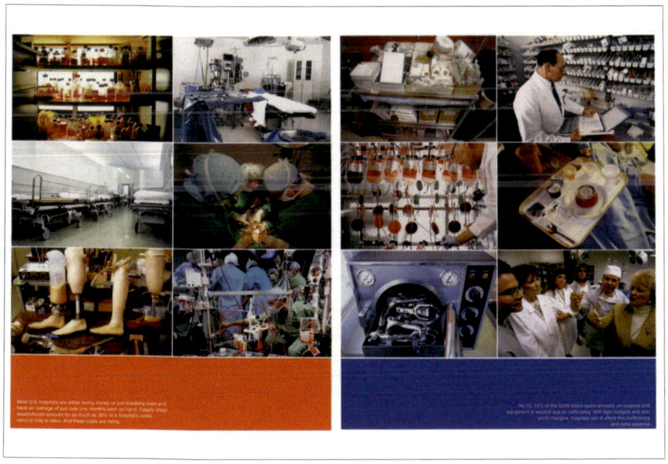

Neoforma

FIRM_ Cahan & Associates
ART DIRECTORS_ Bill Cahan, Sharrie Brooks
DESIGNER_ Sharrie Brooks
PHOTOGRAPHERS_ Graham MacIndoe, Sian Kennedy
COPYWRITER_ Kathy Cooper Parker
PRINTER_ Anderson Lithograph

FIRM_ Casper Design Group
ART DIRECTORS_ Chris Buehler, Bill Aibar
DESIGNER_ Chris Buehler
PHOTOGRAPHERS_ Kingmond Young, Stock
COPYWRITERS_ Steve Goldstein, Chris Buehler, Jim Cas
PRINTER_ Anderson Lithography

COVER PAPER 100lb. Mohawk Navaho Brilliant White Cover
TEXT PAPER 100lb. Mohawk Navaho Brilliant White Text
COLORS 8
PAGES 78

Netflix

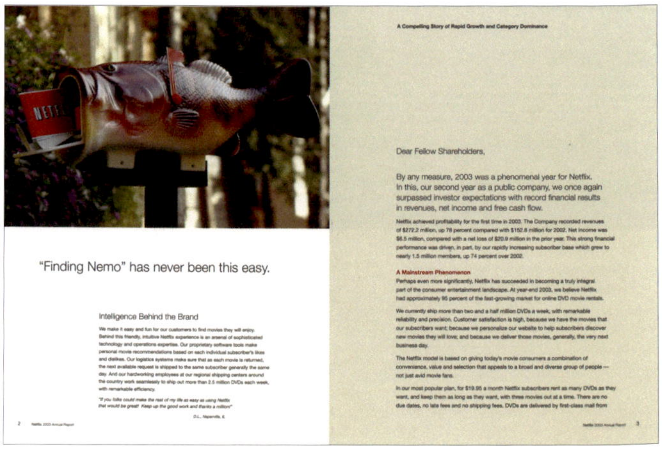

COVER PAPER 100lb. Sappi McCoy Silk Cover
TEXT PAPER 100lb. Sappi McCoy Silk Text
COLORS 7
PAGES 20
QUANTITY 11,000

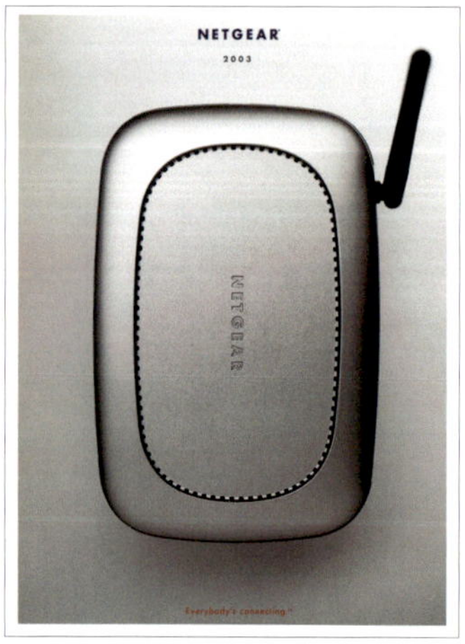

Netgear

FIRM_ Weymouth Design
ART DIRECTOR_ Bob Kellerman
DESIGNERS_ Bob Kellerman, Chi-Wai Song
PHOTOGRAPHERS_ Aida Daay, Anna Weymouth
COPYWRITER_ Netgear
PRINTER_ Colorgraphics

FIRM_ Leimer Cross Design
ART DIRECTOR_ Kerry Leimer
DESIGNER_ Kerry Leimer
PHOTOGRAPHER_ Eric Myer
COPYWRITER_ Stuart H. Clugston
PRINTER_ Frasier Papers

Norske Canada

COVER PAPER 80lb. Pegasus Brilliant White Smooth Cover
TEXT PAPER 100lb. Pegasus Brilliant White Smooth Text
COLORS 8
PAGES 74
QUANTITY 17,000

COVER PAPER 100lb. Dulcet Cover
TEXT PAPER 100lb. Dulcet Text
COLORS 6
PAGES 54
QUANTITY 5,300

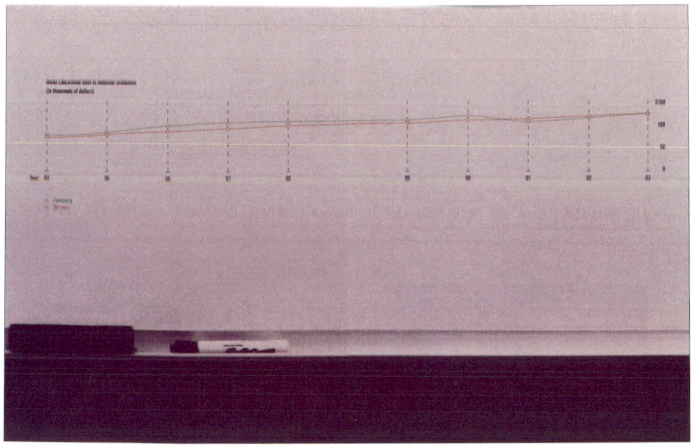

Northwestern University's Feinberg School of Medicine

FIRM_ Pivot Design, Inc.
ART DIRECTORS_ Brock Haldeman, Liz Haldeman
DESIGNERS_ Garrett Bowhall, Jill Kristen Misawa
PHOTOGRAPHER_ Jim Ziv
COPYWRITERS_ Ellen Soo Hoo, Jean Benzies, Laura Bleiler, Sarah A. Meisch, Michael Nyquist, Cheryl Soo Hoo
PRINTER_ Active Graphics

FIRM_ ideas on purpose
ART DIRECTOR_ Darren Namaye
DESIGNER_ Darren Namaye
COPYWRITERS_ Nancy Garfinkel, Heather Ashworth
PRINTER_ Print International

COVER PAPER job parilux
TEXT PAPER job parilux
COLORS 6

Octel Corp.

PacifiCare

FIRM_ Stoyan Design
ART DIRECTORS_ David Stoyan Wooters, Chi Hang
DESIGNER_ Chi Hang
PHOTOGRAPHER_ Wendy Fletcher
COPYWRITER_ Dan Yarbrough
PRINTER_ Colorgraphics

COVER PAPER 80lb. sappi potlach mccoy matte
TEXT PAPER 80lb. sappi potlach mccoy matte
COLORS 8
PAGES 120
QUANTITY 30,000

FIRM_ Howry Design Associates
ART DIRECTOR_ Jill Howry
DESIGNER_ Todd Richards
ILLUSTRATOR_ Liisa Turan
PRINTER_ Color Graphics

Pain Therapeutics

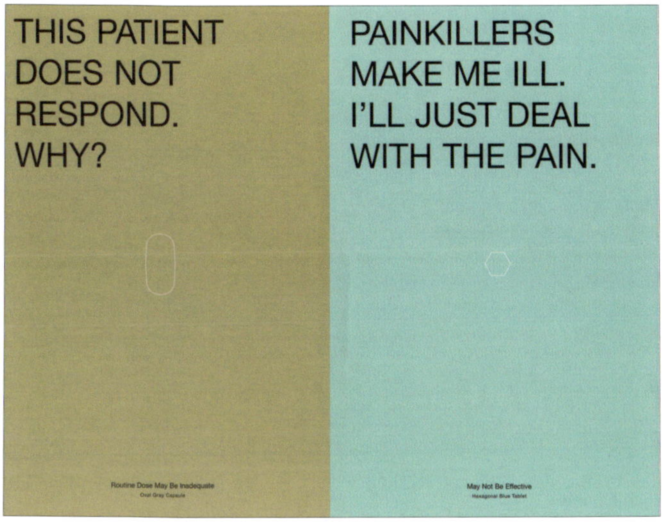

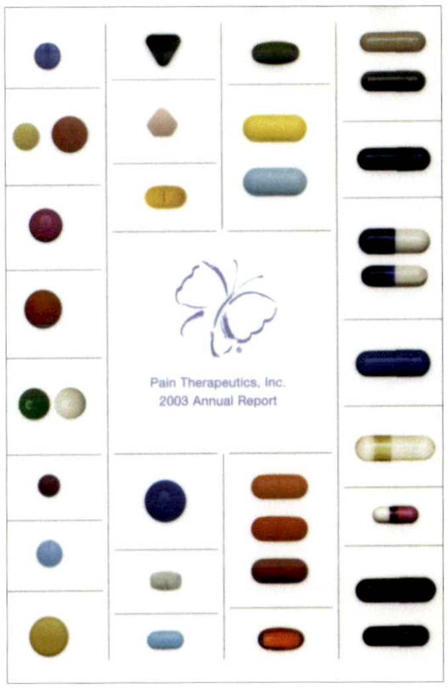

COVER PAPER 130lb. McCoy silk cover
TEXT PAPERS 100lb. McCoy silk text, 62lb. Yupo translucent text
COLORS 6
PAGES 48
QUANTITY 3,000

COVER PAPER 100lb. Glacier opaque text
TEXT PAPER 100lb. Glacier opaque text
COLORS 6
PAGES 40
QUANTITY 2,500

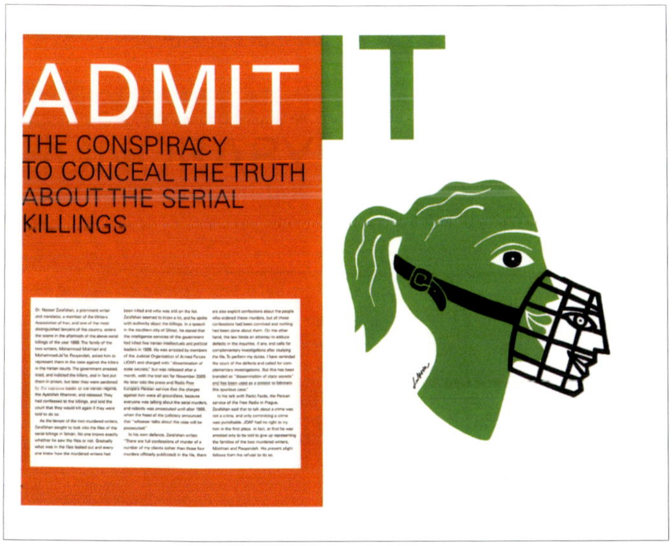

PEN Canada

FIRM_ Soapbox Design Communications Inc.
ART DIRECTOR_ Gary Ocelik
DESIGNER_ Jim Ryce
ILLUSTRATOR_ Luba Lukova
COPYWRITER_ Bert Archer
PRINTER_ Sumerset Graphics Ltd.

FIRM_	Leimer Cross Design
ART DIRECTOR_	Kerry Leimer
DESIGNER_	Kerry Leimer
PHOTOGRAPHERS_	Keith Skelton, Tyler Boley
COPYWRITER_	Jeff Fraga
PRINTER_	Blanchette Press

COVER PAPER 100lb. Domtar Inc. Luna Gloss cover
TEXT PAPERS 80lb. Domtar, Inc. Luna Matte Text, 50lb. Fraser Papers Glacier opaque smooth white
COLORS 8
PAGES 100
QUANTITY 16,000

Pixelworks, Inc.

COVER PAPER 100lb. Domtar titanium cover
TEXT PAPER 80lb. Domtar titanium text
COLORS 6
PAGES 110
QUANTITY 215,000

Plum Creek Timber Company, Inc.

FIRM_	Leonhardt:Fitch
ART DIRECTORS_	Steve Watson, Ray Ueno
DESIGNER_	Steve Watson
PHOTOGRAPHER_	Don Mason Photography
ILLUSTRATORS_	Steve Watson, Charlie Bartlett
COPYWRITER_	Devin Liddell
PRINTER_	GAC Portland

FIRM_ argus
ART DIRECTOR_ stephanie wade
DESIGNER_ stephanie wade
PHOTOGRAPHER_ melgar photography
COPYWRITERS_ ellen brook, stephanie wade
PRINTER_ fong + fong printers

Power Integrations

COVER PAPER 100lb. finch fine bright white cover
TEXT PAPER 100lb. finch fine bright white text
COLORS 5
PAGES 86
QUANTITY 13,000

COVER PAPER 100lb. french smart white cover
TEXT PAPERS 100lb. french smart white text, 70lb. french construction cement green text, 70lb. french construction slate blue text
COLORS 7
PAGES 38
QUANTITY 55,000

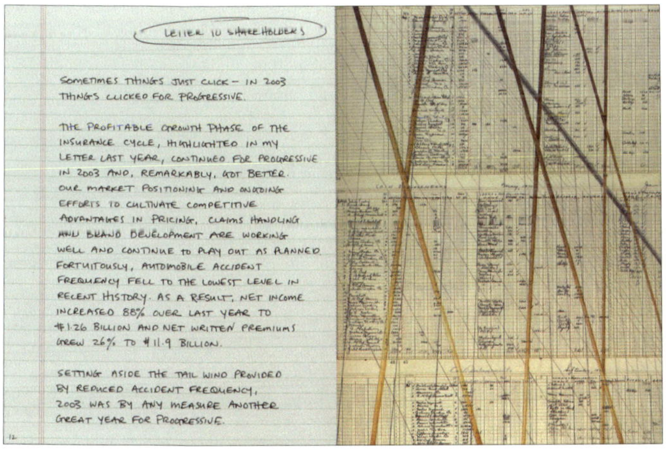

The Progressive Corporation

FIRM_ nesnadny + schwartz: cleveland + new york + toronto
ART DIRECTORS_ joyce nesnadny, mark schwartz
DESIGNERS_ joyce nesnadny, michelle moehler, keith pishnery
ARTIST_ carlos vega
COPYWRITER_ glenn renwick - the progressive corporation
PRINTER_ fortran printing

FIRM_ Merge
ART DIRECTOR_ Ali Harper
DESIGNERS_ Kirk Wells, Chrissie Lein
PHOTOGRAPHER_ Paul Hultberg
COPYWRITER_ David Harrell
PRINTER_ Rainbow Graphics

Project Open Hand/Atlanta

COVER PAPER 80lb. cougar opaque
TEXT PAPERS 80lb. cougar opaque, 70lb. cougar opaque
COLORS 5
PAGES 28
QUANTITY 5,000

COVER PAPER 80lb. stora enso productolith dull
TEXT PAPER 70lb. stora enso productolith dull
COLORS 5
PAGES 128
QUANTITY 120,000

Puget Energy

FIRM_ Thinkhouse Creative
ART DIRECTOR_ Randy Allison
DESIGNER_ Randy Allison
COPYWRITER_ George Bacso
PRINTER_ Quebecor World Acme

FIRM_ Stoyan Design
ART DIRECTORS_ David Stoyan Wooters, Chi Hang
DESIGNER_ Chi Hang
PHOTOGRAPHERS_ Various
PRINTER_ Colorgraphics

Quiksilver

COVER PAPER 60lb. Weyerhaeuser Cougar Text
TEXT PAPER 60lb. Weyerhaeuser Cougar Text
COLORS 8
PAGES 130
QUANTITY 15,000

COVER PAPER Vent Nouvean
TEXT PAPER Vent Nouvean
COLORS 5
PAGES 128
QUANTITY 20,000

Samsung Group

FIRM_ The Corporate Agenda
ART DIRECTORS_ Chris Yun, Daniel Koh, Victor Alvera
PHOTOGRAPHERS_ Ashton Worthington, Leem Jun Bin
COPYWRITER_ Warren Berger
PRINTER_ Samsung Moonhwa Printing Company

FIRM_	methodologie
ART DIRECTOR_	anne traver
DESIGNER_	john rousseau
PHOTOGRAPHERS_	various
COPYWRITERS_	kylie hansen, methodologie, SIA staff
PRINTER_	colorgraphics

COVER PAPER	mohawk navajo cover
TEXT PAPERS	mohawk navajo text, carnival yellow
COLORS	6
PAGES	132
QUANTITY	4,500

Semiconductor Industry Association

COVER PAPER	100lb. sappi mccoy dull cover
TEXT PAPER	100lb. sappi mccoy dull text
COLORS	6
PAGES	38
QUANTITY	10,000

Sesame Workshop

FIRM_	samatamason
ART DIRECTOR_	dave mason
DESIGNER_	beth may
PHOTOGRAPHERS_	victor penner, sesame workshop
COPYWRITERS_	dave mason, gail david, sesame workshop
PRINTER_	blanchette press

FIRM_ cahan & associates
ART DIRECTORS_ bill cahan, michael braley
DESIGNER_ michael braley
PRINTER_ anderson lithograph

Silicon Valley Bank

COVER PAPER 65lb. cougar opaque cover
TEXT PAPER 80lb. mccoy silk text
COLORS 4
PAGES 146

COVER PAPER 65lb. sappi lustro patina cover
TEXT PAPER 80lb. sappi lustro patina text
COLORS 8
PAGES 60
QUANTITY 10,000

Simpletech

FIRM_ stoyan design
ART DIRECTORS_ david stoyan wooters, ryan mahar
DESIGNER_ ryan mahar
PHOTOGRAPHER_ wendy fletcher
PRINTER_ colorgraphics

SITEL Corporation

FIRM_ David Day + Associates
ART DIRECTOR_ David Day
DESIGNER_ Jill Rizzo
PHOTOGRAPHER_ Malone and Company
ILLUSTRATOR_ Jill Rizzo
COPYWRITER_ Nena Grabec
PRINTER_ Omaha Print

COVER PAPER 100lb. Anthem Matte Cover
TEXT PAPER 100lb. Anthem Matte Text
COLORS 6
PAGES 56
QUANTITY 20,000

COVER PAPER 80lb. Cougar Smooth Cover
TEXT PAPERS 65lb. Cougar Smooth Cover, 60lb. Lynx Smooth Book
COLORS 4
PAGES 28
QUANTITY 30,000

SPCA of Texas

FIRM_ RBMM
ART DIRECTORS_ Steve Gibbs, Dick Mitchell, Brian Boyd
DESIGNER_ Brian Owens
ILLUSTRATOR_ David Vaught
PHOTOGRAPHERS_ Peter Kao (cover), Joe Grisham, Chris Whalen, Mark Bumgarner, John Wong, Robie Capps, Tadd Myers, Heather Ezell
COPYWRITERS_ David Culp, Kathy Edwards
PRINTER_ Williamson Printing Corporation

FIRM_ starbucks creative group
ART DIRECTOR_ doug keyes
DESIGNER_ doug keyes
PHOTOGRAPHER_ leslie williamson
COPYWRITER_ anna david
PRINTER_ graphic arts center

Starbucks Corporation

COVER PAPER fraser custom
TEXT PAPER fraser custom
COLORS 5
PAGES 40
QUANTITY 275,000

COVER PAPER 80lb. gilbert paper oxford vellum profit
TEXT PAPERS smart papers kromekote 6pt. c2s, 80lb. gilbert paper oxford vellum road text, 70lb. smart papers carnival soft white vellum text
COLORS 6
PAGES 106
QUANTITY 17,000

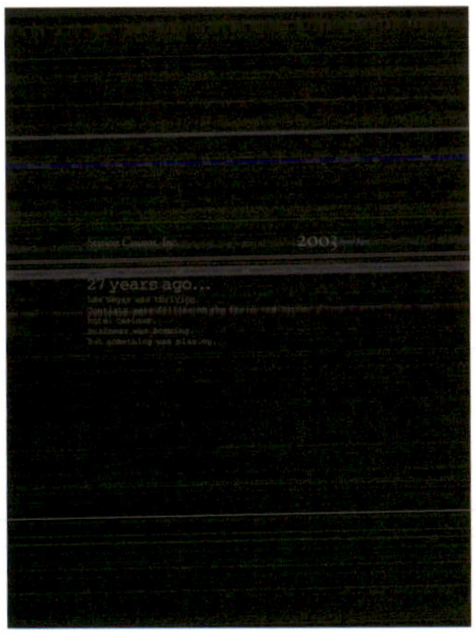

Station Casinos, Inc.

FIRM_ kuhlmann leavitt, inc.
ART DIRECTOR_ deanna kuhlmann-leavitt
DESIGNERS_ deanna kuhlmann-leavitt, monica goldsburg, tom twellman
PHOTOGRAPHERS_ gregg goldman, everard williams jr., cameron davidson
PRINTER_ hennegan printing co.

FIRM_	samatamason
ART DIRECTORS_	Greg Samata, Kevin Krueger
DESIGNERS_	Kevin Krueger, Skot Waldron
PHOTOGRAPHERS_	Greg Samata, Chris Kirzeder
COPYWRITER_	Tony Leighton
PRINTER_	Blanchette Press

Tandberg

COVER PAPER	100lb. Sappi Hanno Art Silk Cover
TEXT PAPER	80lb. Fraser Papers Glacier Opaque Text
COLORS	8
PAGES	74
QUANTITY	8,500

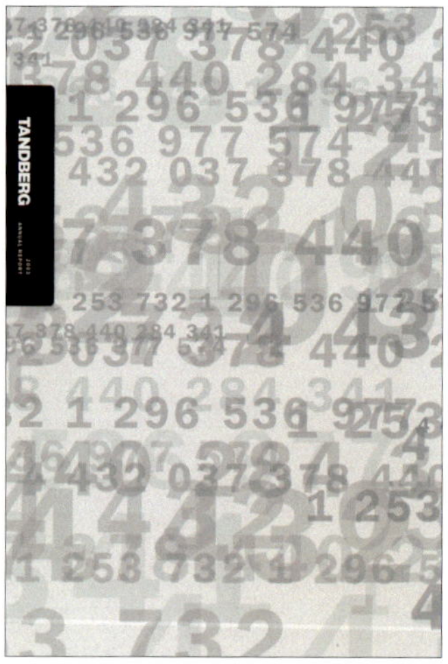

COVER PAPER	70lb. Finch Opaque Creme Text
TEXT PAPER	70lb. Finch Opaque Creme Smooth
COLORS	2
PAGES	32
QUANTITY	1,500

Turn Around

FIRM_	Spur Design
ART DIRECTOR_	David Plunkert
DESIGNERS_	Kurt Seidle, David Plurkert
ILLUSTRATOR_	David Plunkert
COPYWRITER_	Shelly Apple - Terranova
PRINTER_	Advance Printing

FIRM_ VSA Partners
ART DIRECTOR_ Curt Schreiber
DESIGNERS_ Kevin Hughes, Michelle Platts
PHOTOGRAPHER_ Misha Gravenor
PRINTER_ Sandy Alexander

Tyco

COVER PAPER 100lb. Mohawk Options white smooth cover
TEXT PAPER 80lb. Mohawk Options white smooth text
COLORS 8
PAGES 128
QUANTITY 1,200,000

COVER PAPER 24W Fraser Synergy white smooth
TEXT PAPERS 24W Fraser Synergy white smooth, 30lb. Unisource Newsprint
COLORS 5
PAGES 74
QUANTITY 5,000

University of Calgary

FIRM_ Sasges Wright Inc.
ART DIRECTORS_ Hila Sasges, Isabel Abdai
DESIGNER_ Isabel Abdai
PHOTOGRAPHER_ Maja Swannie
COPYWRITER_ Terry Bullick
PRINTER_ Blanchette Press

FIRM_ And Partners, NY
ART DIRECTOR_ David Schimmel
DESIGNER_ Susan Brzozowski
PHOTOGRAPHER_ Vincent Ricardel
COPYWRITER_ Ryan Poliakoff
PRINTER_ Finlay

VF Corporation

COVER PAPER 100lb. Mohawk Bluewhite
TEXT PAPERS 80lb. Mohawk Bluewhite, 70lb. Mohawk Opaque Vellum
COLORS 7
PAGES 102
QUANTITY 60,000

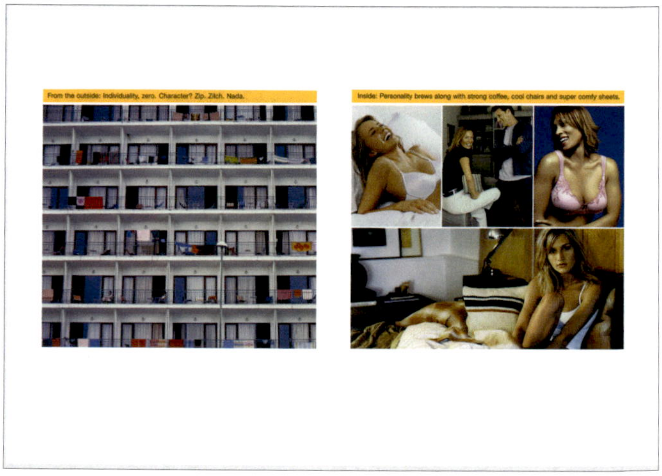

COVER PAPER 80lb. Utopia II Matte
TEXT PAPER 80lb. Utopia II Matte
COLORS 7
PAGES 80
QUANTITY 25,000

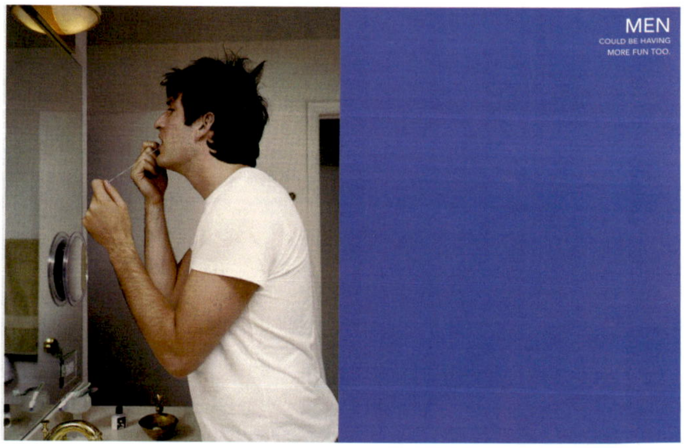

Vivus Inc.

FIRM_ Howry Design Associates
ART DIRECTOR_ Jill Howry
DESIGNER_ Ty Whittington
PHOTOGRAPHER_ Stock
PRINTER_ Waller Press

FIRM_	Russell Design
ART DIRECTOR_	Anthony Russell
DESIGNER_	Julie Beard
ILLUSTRATOR_	Dave Lesh
COPYWRITER_	Lindsay Beaman
PRINTER_	Sandy Alexander

WP Stewart

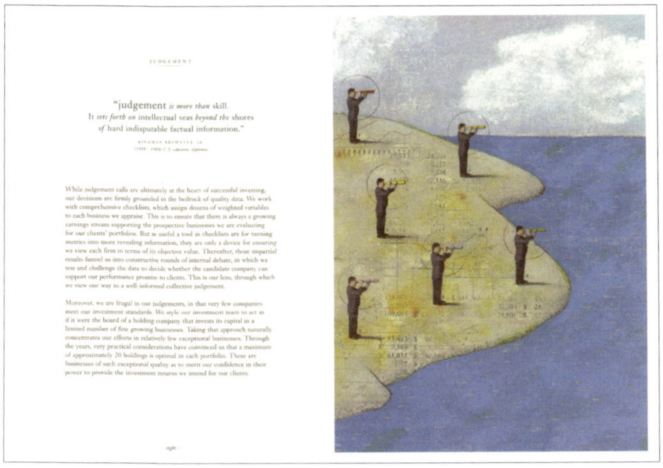

COVER PAPER	100lb. Monadnock Astrolite Cover
TEXT PAPER	100lb. Monadnock Astrolite Text
COLORS	7
PAGES	46
QUANTITY	9,000

COVER PAPER	100lb. New Leaf Pax
TEXT PAPER	80lb. New Leaf Pax
COLORS	6
PAGES	44
QUANTITY	22,000

WD40

FIRM_	Turner & Associates
ART DIRECTORS_	Laurie Carrigan, Steve Turner
DESIGNER_	Laura Milton
PHOTOGRAPHER_	Jock McDonald
COPYWRITER_	Brad Londy
PRINTER_	Anderson Lithograph

Weyerhaeuser Company

FIRM_ Leonhardt:Fitch
ART DIRECTORS_ Ray Ueno, Lesley Feldman
DESIGNER_ Lesley Feldman
PHOTOGRAPHERS_ Gary Darby, Dave Putnam
ILLUSTRATOR_ Ning Yeh
COPYWRITERS_ Devin Liddell, Xan McCallum, Bruce Amundson
PRINTER_ GAC Portland

COVER PAPER 100lb. Weyerhaeuser opaque cream cover
TEXT PAPER 70lb. Weyerhaeuser opaque cream text
COLORS 6
PAGES 90
QUANTITY 160,000

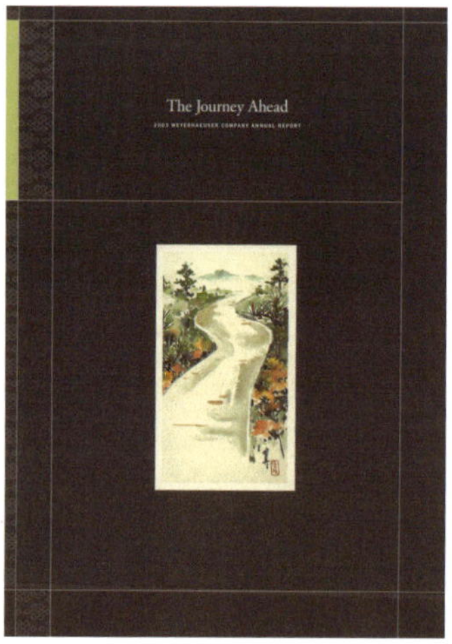

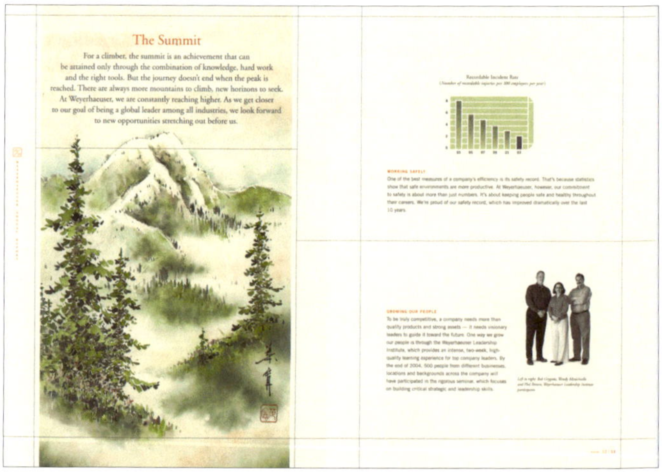

COVER PAPER 130lb. Mohawk super fine
TEXT PAPERS 70lb. Strathmore opaque, 130lb. Mohawk superfine
COLORS 8
PAGES 40
QUANTITY 53,000

XOMA

FIRM_ Howry Design Associates
ART DIRECTOR_ Jill Howry
DESIGNER_ Ty Whittington
PHOTOGRAPHER_ Robert Schlatter
ILLUSTRATOR_ Liisa Turan
PRINTER_ Graphic Press

FIRM_	cahan & associates
ART DIRECTORS_	bill cahan, craig williamson
DESIGNER_	craig williamson
PHOTOGRAPHERS_	todd hido, ron coppock-king
COPYWRITER_	tony leighton
PRINTER_	lithographix

Yellow

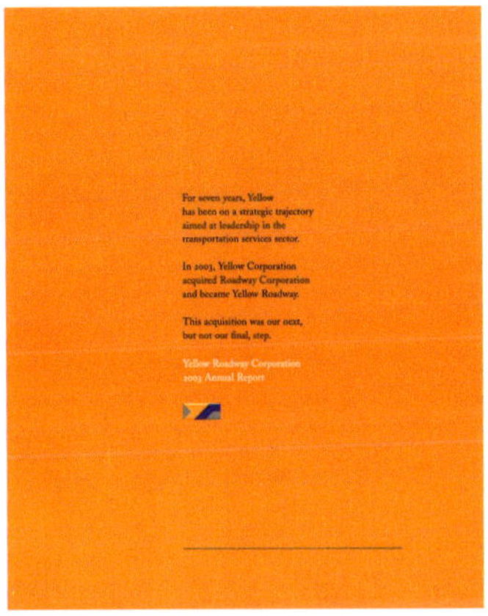

COVER PAPER	80lb. sterling matte cover
TEXT PAPERS	70lb. sterling matte text, 60lb. sterling matte
COLORS	8
PAGES	86
QUANTITY	30,000

TEXT PAPER	150g. luxosatin
PAGES	108
QUANTITY	5,000

Zumtobel AG

FIRM_	sagmeister inc.
ART DIRECTOR	stefan sagmeister
DESIGNER_	matthias ernstberger
PHOTOGRAPHER_	bela borsodi
COPYWRITER_	otto riewoldt
PRINTER_	veronaprint; cover: zumtobel staff, reiss international

CORPORATIONS

Aber Diamond Corporation
page 252
250 University Avenue
Toronto, Ontario M5H 3E5 Canada
p (416) 362-2237
f (416) 362-2230
www.aber.ca

Adobe Systems Inc.
page 252
345 Park Avenue
MS A12-500
San Jose, CA 95110
p (408) 536-4811
f (408) 537-6160
www.adobe.com

Alberta Ballet
pages 180-181, 204, 253
141 18 Avenue SW
Calgary, Alberta T2S 0B8 Canada
p (403) 245-4222
f (403) 245-6573
www.albertaballet.com

Alexandria Real Estate Equities
pages 205, 216, 253
135 North Los Robles Avenue
Suite 250
Pasadena, CA 91101
p (626) 396-4828
f (626) 578-0770
www.labspace.com

Allstate
page 254
2775 Sanders Road
Northbrook, IL 60062
p (847) 402-5600
f (847) 326-7519

AltaLink
page 254
Box 20 Station M
Calgary, Alberta T2P 2G9 Canada
p (403) 267-2176
f (403) 267-3454
www.altalink.ca

AMB Property Corporation
page 255
Pier 1 Bay 1
San Francisco, CA 94111
p (415) 394-9000
f (415) 394-9001

American Vanguard
page 255
4695 MacArthur Court
Newport Beach, CA 92660
p (949) 260-1200
www.amvac-chemical.com

AptarGroup
page 256
475 West Terra Cotta Avenue
Suite E
Crystal Lake, IL 60014
p (815) 477-0424
f (815) 477-0481
www.aptargroup.com

Arcis Corporation
pages 228, 256
300, 404 6th Avenue SW
Calgary, Alberta T2P 0R9 Canada
p (403) 781-1700
f (403) 269-1966
www.arcis.com

Avery Dennison
page 257
150 North Orange Grove Boulevard
Pasadena, CA 91103
p (626) 304-2014
f (626) 577-9587

BP
pages 192, 229, 257
1 St. James Square
London, SW1Y 4PD England
p 44-207-496-4159

BRE Properties, Inc.
page 258
44 Montgomery Street
36th Floor
San Francisco, CA 94104-5525
p (415) 445-6530
f (415) 445-6505

Brunswick Corporation
page 258
1 North Field Court
Lake Forest, IL 60045-4811
p (847) 735-4700
f (847) 735-4359
www.brunswick.com

Burlington Northern Santa Fe
pages 240, 259
2650 Lou Menk Drive
Fort Worth, TX 76131
p (817) 867-6411
www.bnsf.com

Cabot Corporation
page 259
2 Seaport Lane
Boston, MA 02210
p (617) 342-6318
f (617) 342-6312
www.cabot-corp.com

calavo growers inc.
page 260
2530 red hill avenue
santa ana, CA 92705
p (949) 833-4201
f (949) 660-4232
www.calavo.com

calgary exhibition & stampede
pages 206,260
box 1060 station M
calgary, alberta T2P 2K8 canada
p (403) 261-0110
f (403) 264-0299
www.calgarystampede.com

casey house foundation
page 261
119 isabella street
toronto, ontario M4Y 1P2 canada
p (416) 962-7600
f (416) 962-5147

CEC entertainment
page 261
4441 west airport freeway
irving, TX 75062
p (972) 258-4222
f (972) 258-5619
www.chuckecheese.com

cell therapeutics, inc.
page 262
501 elliot avenue west
seattle, WA 98119
p (206) 282-7100
f (206) 284-6206
www.ctiseattle.com

charles schwab
page 262
120 kearny
san francisco, CA 94104
p (415) 627-7000
f (415) 636-5970

chelsea property group
page 263
103 eisenhower parkway
roseland, NJ 07068
p (973) 228-6111
f (973) 228-3518
www.cpgi.com

chicago volunteer legal services
pages 193,263
100 north lasalle street
suite 900
chicago, IL 60602
p (312) 332-5542
f (312) 332-1460
www.cvls.org

children's home and aid society
pages 194,264
125 south wacker
14th floor
chicago, IL 60606
p (312) 424-6812
f (312) 424-0056
www.chasi.org

coca-cola femsa
pages 217,264
guillermo gonzalez camarena
NO. 600, col centro de ciudad
santa fe 02110 mexico
p 52-5081-5120
f 52-5292-3474
www.cocacola-femsa.com.mx

cost plus world market
pages 195,241,265
200 4th street
oakland, CA 94607
p (510) 893-7300
f (510) 465-6805
www.costplus.com

courier corporation
pages 196,230,242,265
15 wellmann avenue
north chelmsford, MA 01863
p (978) 251-6000
f (978) 251-0976
www.courier.com

entravision communications
pages 218,266
2425 olympic boulevard
suite 600
west santa monica, CA 90404
p (310) 447-3870
f (310) 449-1306
info@entravision.com
www.entravision.com

expeditors international of washington, inc.
page 266
1015 third avenue
12th floor
seattle, WA 98104
p (206) 674-3400
f (206) 674-3459

fedex
page 267
942 south shady grove road
memphis, TN 38120
p (901) 818-7037
www.fedex.com

first data corporation
pages 219,267
6200 south quebec street
greenwood village, CO 80111
p (800) 735-3362
www.firstdata.com

first health
pages 220,268
3200 highland avenue
downers grove, IL 60515-1282
p (630) 737-8900
f (630) 737-7856

first industrial realty trust, inc.
page 268
311 south wacker drive
suite 4000
chicago, IL 60606
p (312) 344-4320
f (312) 922-6320
www.firstindustrial.com

first state bancorporation
page 269
7900 jefferson NE
albuquerue, NM 87109
p (505) 241-7615

the fresh air fund
page 269
633 third avenue
14th floor
new york, NY 10017
p (212) 897-8800
f (212) 897-0003

GATX
page 270
500 west monroe street
chicago, IL 60661
p (800) 428-8161
f (312) 621-6648
www.gatx.com

gay men's health crisis
page 270
119 west 24th street
9th floor
new york, NY 10011
p (212) 367 1210
fax (212) 367-1112
www.gmhc.org

the george gund foundation
pages 243,271
1845 guildhall building
45 prospect avenue
cleveland, OH 44115
p (216) 241-3114
f (216) 241-6560
www.gundfdn.org

GLSEN
page 271
121 west 27th street
suite 804
new york, NY 10001
p (212) 727-0135
f (212) 727-0254
www.glsen.org

Greater Bay Area Make-A-Wish Foundation
page 278
120 Montgomery street
suite 1080
san Francisco, CA 94104
p (415) 982-9474
www.makeawish.org

Greater Bay Bancorp
pages 197,231,272
430 cowper street
Palo Alto, CA 94301
p (925) 743-9200

Greater Phoenix Economic council
page 272
Two North central Avenue
suite 2500
Phoenix, AZ 85004
p (602) 262-8625

Harley-Davidson
pages 232,273
3700 west Juneau Avenue
Milwaukee, WI 53208
p (414) 343-8300
f (414) 343-4806
www.harley-davidson.com

Headwaters Fund
page 273
122 west Franklin Avenue
Minneapolis, MN 55404
p (612) 879-0602
f (612) 879-0613
www.headwatersfoundation.org

Herman Miller, Inc.
page 274
855 East Main Avenue
suite 162
zeeland, MI 49464
p (888) 443-4357
f (616) 654-8210
www.hermanmiller.com

IBM
pages 274-275
New orchard Road
Armonk, NY 10504
p (914) 499-5621
f (914) 499-7642
www.ibm.com

IMS Health Inc.
page 275
1499 Post Road
Fairfield, CT 06430
p (203) 319-4772
www.imshealth.com

InterDigital communications corporation
page 276
781 Third Avenue
King of Prussia, PA 19406
p (610) 878-7815
f (610) 878-7842
www.interdigal.com

Intrawest corporation
pages 182-183,221,276
200 Burrand street
suite 800
vancouver, British columbia
V6C 3L6 canada
p (604) 669-9777
f (604) 669-0605
www.intrawest.com

iStar Financial
pages 207,244,277
1114 Avenue of the Americas
New York, NY 10036
p (212) 930-9400
f (212) 930-9494
www.istarfinancial.com

KB Home
page 277
10990 Wilshire Boulevard
7th Floor
Los Angeles, CA 90024
p (310) 231-4000
f (310) 231-4250
www.kbhome.com

Kenneth cole Productions, Inc.
page 278
603 west 50th street
New York, NY 10016
p (212) 830-7446

Manpower, Inc.
page 279
5301 North Ironwood Road
Milwaukee, WI 53201
p (414) 961-1000
f (414) 961-8780
www.manpower.com

Marguerite casey Foundation
pages 184-185,198,208,233,279
1300 Dexter Avenue North
seattle, WA 98109
p (206) 691-3134
f (206) 286-2725
www.caseygrants.org

Maxygen
page 280
200 Penobscot Drive
Redwood city, CA 94063
p (650) 298-5300
f (650) 298-5877

The McGraw-Hill companies
page 280
1221 Avenue of the Americas
New York, NY 10020
p (212) 512-4495
f (212) 512-2703
www.mcgraw-hill.com

Mentor corporation
pages 222,281
201 Mentor Drive
santa Barbara, CA 93111
p (805) 879-6000
f (805) 967-3362
www.mentorcorp.com

Mercury General corporation
page 281
4484 wilshire Boulevard
Los Angeles, CA 90010
p (323) 937-1060
f (323) 857-7116
www.mercuryinsurance.com

MFI
pages 174-175,209,282
333 The Hyde
Edgware Road
London, England NW9 6TD
p 44-208-913-5447
f 44-208-913-5181
www.mfi.co.uk

Microsoft corporation
page 282
one Microsoft way
Redmond, WA 98052
p (425) 882-8080
f (425) 936-7329
www.microsoft.com

Nabors Industries
page 283
515 west Greens Road #1200
Houston, TX 77067
p (281) 874-0035
f (281) 775-8195
www.nabors.com

Neoforma
pages 234,283
3061 zanker Road
san Jose, CA 95134
p (408) 468-4000
f (408) 468-4045

Netflix
page 284
970 University Avenue
Los Gatos, CA 95032
p (408) 317-3700
www.netflix.com

Netgear
Page 284
4500 Great America Parkway
Santa Clara, CA 95054
p (408) 907-8000
f (408) 907-8097
www.netgear.com

Norske Canada
Page 285
250 Howe Street
Vancouver, British Columbia
Canada V6C 3A8
p (604) 654-4319
f (604) 654-4070
www.norskecanada.com

Northwestern University's
Feinberg School of Medicine
Page 285
303 East Chicago Avenue
Chicago, IL 60611
p (312) 503-8618
f (312) 503-0146
www.feinberg.northwestern.edu

Octel Corporation
Page 286
Global House
Bailey Lane
Manchester M90 4AA
United Kingdom
p 44-161-498-8889
f 44-161-498-1899

PacifiCare
Page 286
5995 Plaza Drive
Cypress, CA 90630
p (800) 631-0969
f (714) 226-3581
www.pacificare.com

Pain Therapeutics
Pages 235,245,287
416 Browning Way
South San Francisco, CA 94080
p (650) 624-8200
f (650) 624-8222
www.paintrails.com

PEN Canada
Pages 223,236,287
24 Ryerson Avenue
Toronto, Ontario M5T 2P3 Canada
p (416) 703-8448
f (416) 703-3870
www.pencanada.ca

Pixelworks
Page 288
8100 SW Nyberg Road
Tualatin, OR 97062
p (503) 454-1742

Plum Creek Timber Company, Inc.
Page 288
999 Third Avenue
Suite 4300
Seattle, WA 98101
p (206) 467-3600
f (206) 467-3797
www.plumcreek.com

Power Integrations
Page 289
5245 Hellyer Avenue
San Jose, CA 95138
p (408) 414-9200
www.powerint.com

The Progressive Corporation
Pages 224,289
6300 Wilson Mills Road
Mayfield Village, OH 44143
p (440) 446-7930
f (440) 446-7168
www.progressive.com

Project Open Hand/Atlanta
Page 290
176 Ottley Drive NE
Atlanta, GA 30324
p (404) 872-8089
www.projectopenhand.org

Puget Energy
Page 290
PO BOX 97034
Bellevue, WA 98009
p (425) 462-3206
f (425) 462-3301
www.pse.com

Quiksilver
Pages 186-187,210,246,291
15202 Graham Street
Huntington Beach, CA 92649
p (714) 889-2200
f (714) 889-2322
www.quiksilver.com

Samsung Group
Pages 211,247,291
736-1 Hannan
2 Dong
Yongsan-Gu, Seoul 140-739
Korea
p 82-2-3780-3576

Semiconductor Industry
Association
Page 292
181 Metro Drive
Suite 450
San Jose, CA 95110
p (408) 436-6600
f (408) 436-6646
www.sia-online.org

Sesame Workshop
Page 292
1 Lincoln Plaza
New York, NY 10023
p (212) 595-3456
www.sesameworkshop.org

Silicon Valley Bank
Pages 237,293
185 Berry Street
Suite 3000
San Francisco, CA 94107
p (408) 654-7400
f (408) 496-9927

SimpleTech
Pages 199,293
3001 Daimler Street
Santa Ana, CA 92705
p (949) 260-8328
f (949) 417-0609
www.simpletech.com

SITEL Corporation
Pages 188-189,294
7277 World Communications Drive
Omaha, NE 68122
p (402) 963-6810
www.sitel.com

SPCA of Texas
Pages 178-179,248,294
362 South Industrial Boulevard
Dallas, TX 75207
p (214) 651-9611
f (214) 651-9244
www.spca.org

Starbucks Corporation
Page 295
2401 Utah Avenue South
8th Floor
Seattle, WA 98134
p (206) 318-8144
f (206) 682-9051
www.starbucks.com

Station Casinos, Inc.
Page 295
PO BOX 29500
Las Vegas, NV 89126
p (702) 367-2411
www.stationcasinos.com

Tandberg
Page 296
651 West Washington Street
Suite 401
Chicago, IL 60661
p (312) 961-4565
f (312) 798-8594
www.tandberg.net

Turn Around
Pages 225, 296
401 Washington Avenue
Towson, MD 21204
p (410) 377-8111
f (410) 377-6806
www.turnaroundinc.org

Tyco
Page 297
9 Roszel Road
Princeton, NJ 08540
p (609) 720-4200
f (609) 720-4208
www.tyco.com

University of Calgary
Page 297
2500 University Drive NW
Calgary, Alberta T2N 1N4 Canada
p (403) 220-2720
f (403) 220-4361
www.ucalgary.ca

VF Corporation
Page 298
105 Corporate Center Boulevard
Greensboro, NC 27408
p (336) 424-6189
www.vfc.com

Vivus Inc.
Pages 200, 212, 298
1172 Castro Street
Mountain View, CA 94040
p (650) 934-5200
f (650) 934-5209
www.vivus.com

WD40
Pages 176-177, 299
1061 Cudahy Place
San Diego, CA 92110
p (619) 275-1400
f (619) 275-5823
www.wd40.com

Weyerhaeuser Company
Page 300
3810 Weyerhaeuser Way South
Federal Way, WA 98063
p (253) 924-2345
www.weyerhaeuser.com

WP Stewart
Page 299
Trinity Hall
43 Cedar Avenue
Hamilton, Bermuda HM12
p 441-294-4429
f 441-296-6823
www.wpstewart.com

XOMA
Page 300
2910 Seventh Street
Berkeley, CA 94710
p (510) 204-7200
www.xoma.com

Yellow
Page 301
10990 Roe Avenue
Overland Park, KS 66211
p (913) 696-6100
f (913) 344-4720

Zumtobel AG
Pages 172-173, 201, 213, 249, 301
Hochsterstrasse 8
6850 Dornbien, Austria
p 43-5572-509-575
f 43-5572-390-602

Addison
Pages 207,244,257,270,277,280
20 Exchange Place
18th Floor
New York, NY 10005
p (212) 229-5000
f (212) 929-3010
www.addison.com

And Partners, NY
Page 298
156 Fifth Avenue #1234
New York, NY 10010
p (212) 414-4700
f (212) 414-2915
www.andpartnersny.com

Argus
Pages 278,289
531 Howard Street #2
San Francisco, CA 94105
p (415) 247-2800
f (415) 247-2803
www.argussf.com

BaileyCo-NYC
Page 270
82 East 3rd Street, #5A
New York, NY 10003
p (212) 253-8458
f (212) 253-8458
baileyco@bway.net

BHI
Pages 258,268
118 North Aberdeen Street
Chicago, IL 60607
p (312) 850-2041
f (312) 850-0033
www.bhi1.com

Cahan & Associates
Pages 197,231,234,258,272,280,283,293,301
171 2nd Street
5th Floor
San Francisco, CA 94105
p (415) 621-0915
f (415) 621 7642
info@cahanassociates.com
www.cahanassociates.com

Campbell Sheffield Design
Page 261
130 Spadina Boulevard
Suite 801
Toronto, Ontario M5V 2L4 Canada
p (416) 504-0144
f (416) 504-0304
www.campbellsheffield.com

Casper Design Group
Page 284
2105 Martin Luther King Junior Way
Berkeley, CA 94704
p (510) 859-0200
f (510) 859-0210
www.casperdesign.com

CMG Design Inc.
Page 281
500 South Raymond Avenue
Pasadena, CA 91105
p (626) 395-0888
f (626) 395-0899
www.cmgdesign.com

Corporate Agenda
Pages 211,247,291
311 West 43rd Street
7th Floor
New York, NY 10036
p (212) 582-6200
f (212) 582-2747
www.corporateagenda.com

Curran & Connors, Inc.
Page 278
333 Marcus Boulevard
Hauppauge, NY 11788-2001
p (516) 435-0400
f (516) 435-1604

David Day & Associates
Pages 188-189,294
1207 South 75th Street
Omaha, NE 68124
p (402) 398-1108
f (402) 398-1492
www.dday.com

Douglas Joseph Partners
Pages 218,266
11812 San Vicente Boulevard
Suite 125
Los Angeles, CA 90049
p (310) 440-3100
f (310) 440-3103
info@djpartners.com
www.djpartners.com

EAI/Atlanta
Page 267
1000 Northyards Boulevard
Round House, Suite 100
Atlanta, GA 30313
p (404) 614-4299
f (404) 614-4288
www.eai-atl.com

Eleven Inc.
Page 255
445 Bush Street
San Francisco, CA 94108
p (415) 707-1111
f (415) 707-1100
www.eleveninc.com

Fervor Creative
Page 272
7038 East Osborn Road
Scottsdale, AZ 85251
p (480) 970-1400
f (480) 429-8577
www.fervorcreative.com

Garfinkel
Page 144
115 Cedar Springs Drive
Athens, GA 30605
p (706) 369-6831
f (706) 369-1761
info@garfinkeldesign.com
www.garfinkeldesign.com

Herman Miller (In House Design)
Page 274
855 East Main Avenue
Suite 162
Zeeland, MI 49464
p (888) 443-4357
f (616) 654-8210
www.hermanmiller.com

Highwood Communications Ltd.
Pages 206,260
300 1210 8th Street SW
Calgary, Alberta T2R 1L3 Canada
p (403) 244-6313
f (403) 245-4048

Howry Design Associates
Pages 200,212,235,245,287,
298,300
354 Pine Street
Suite 600
San Francisco, CA 94104
p (415) 433-2035
f (415) 433-0816
www.howry.com

Ideas On Purpose
Page 286
27 West 20th Street
Suite 1001
New York, NY 10001
p (212) 366-6355
f (212) 366-6353
www.ideasonpurpose.com

Kuhlmann Leavitt, Inc.
Page 295
7810 Forsyth Boulevard
Suite 2W
St. Louis, MO 63105
p (314) 725-6616
f (314) 725-6618
www.kuhlmannleavitt.com

Leimer Cross Design
Pages 266,285,288
12 Aulii Drive
Makawao Maui, HI 96768
p (808) 572-2382
f (808) 572-2382
www.leimercross.com

Leonhardt: Fitch
pages 262,282,288,300
1218 Third Avenue
suite 620
seattle, WA 98101
p (206) 624-0551
f (206) 624-0875
www.leonhardt-fitch.com

Louey/Rubino Design Group Inc.
page 277
2525 Main street
suite 204
santa Monica, CA 90405
p (310) 396-7724
f (310) 396-1686
www.loueyrubino.com

Lowercase, Inc.
pages 193,263
213 west Institute Plaza
suite 311
chicago, IL 60610
p (312) 274-0652
f (312) 274-0659
info@lowercaseinc.com
www.lowercaseinc.com

McNulty & company
pages 222,260,281
3064 Foothill Drive
Thousand oaks, CA 91361
p (805) 381-1852
f (805) 381-1862
www.mcnultyco.com

Merge
page 290
884 Monroe Drive
Atlanta, GA 30308
p (404) 724-4942
f (404) 724-0141
www.mergeagency.com

Meta 4 Design, Inc.
page 254
311 west superior street
suite 504
chicago, IL 60610
p (312) 337-4674
f (312) 337-3687
www.meta4design.com

MetaDesign
page 252
350 Pacific Avenue
suite 300
san Francisco, CA 94111
p (415) 627-0790
f (415) 627-0795
www.metadesign.com

Methodologie, Inc.
pages 184-185,198,208,233,
240,259,279,292
808 Howell street
6th Floor
seattle, WA 98101
p (206) 623-1044
f (206) 625-0154
info@methodologie.com
www.methodologie.com

Nesnadny + Schwartz
pages 243,271,289
10803 Magnolia Drive
cleveland, OH 44106
p (216) 791-7721
f (216) 791-9560
info@NSideas.com
www.NSideas.com

NU
pages 180-181,204,253
31511 21 Avenue SW
calgary, Alberta T2T 0M8 canada
p (403) 512-7298
f (403) 245-4048

OPTO Design
pages 205,216,253
214 sullivan street, #6C
New York, NY 10012
p (212) 254-4470
f (212) 254-5266
www.optodesign.com

Paragraphs Design
pages 217,264
329 west 18th street
suite 801
chicago, IL 60616
p (312) 828-0200
f (312) 828-9888
www.paragraphs.com

Petrick Design
pages 220,268
3701 North Ravenswood Avenue
suite 248
chicago, IL 60613
p (773) 296-6610
f (773) 296-6405

Pivot Design, Inc.
page 285
230 west Huron street
4th Floor
chicago, IL 60610-3620
p (312) 787-7707
f (312) 787-7737
staff@pivotdesign.com
www.pivotdesign.com

RBMM
pages 178-179,248,294
7007 Twin Hills
suite 200
Dallas, TX 75231-5184
p (214) 987-6500
f (214) 987-3662
www.rbmm.com

Result Inc.
page 254
2219 4th street SW
calgary, Alberta T2S 1X1 canada
p (403) 237-9669
f (403) 237-6626
www.resultinc.com

Russell Design
page 299
588 Broadway #307
New York, NY 10012
p (212) 431-8770
f (212) 431-8771
www.russelldesign.com

Sagmeister Inc
pages 172-173,201,213,249,301
222 west 14th street #15A
New York, NY 10011
p (212) 647-1789
f (212) 647-1788
www.sagmeister.com

SamataMason
pages182183,194,221,256,264,276,
279,292,296
101 south First street
Dundee, IL 60118
p (847) 428-8600
f (847) 428-6564
www.samatamason.com

SAS
pages 174-175,209,282
6 salem Road
London W2 4BU England
p 44-207-243-3232
f 44-207-243-3216
www.sasdesign.co.uk

SasgesWright Inc.
pages 228,256,297
888, 10th street SW
calgary, Alberta T2P 2X1 canada
p (403) 262-9323
f (403) 262-9399
www.sasgeswright.com

Savage Design Group, Inc.
page 283
4203 Yoakum Boulevard
4th Floor
Houston, TX 77006
p (713) 522-1555
f (713) 522-1582
www.savagedesign.com

sequel studio
pages 263,275
12 west 27th street
15th floor
New York, NY 10001
p (212) 994-4320
f (646) 935-0582
www.sequelstudio.com

Linda sherman Design
page 146
9825 canal Road
Montgomery village, MD 20886
p (301) 590-0604
f (301) 590-0605
linda@lshermandesign.com
wwwlshermandesign.com

soapbox Design communications Inc.
pages 223,236,287
187 King street E
3rd floor
Toronto, ontario M5A 1J5 canada
p (416) 920-2099
f (416) 920-8178
www.soapboxdesign.com

spur Design
pages 225,296
3504 Ash street
Baltimore, MD 21211
p (410) 235-7803
f (410) 235-4674
www.spurdesign.com

squires & company
pages 261,269
2913 canton street
Dallas, TX 75226
p (214) 939-9194
f (214) 939-3464
www.squirescompany.com

starbucks creative Group
page 295
2401 utah Avenue south
8th floor
seattle, WA 98134
p (206) 318-8144
f 206) 682-9051
www.starbucks.com

stoyan Design
pages 186-
187,199,210,246,255,286,291,293
2482 Newport Boulevard
suite 8
costa Mesa, CA 92627
p (949) 631-6314
f (949) 631-6611
www.stoyandesign.com

suka Design
pages 145,269,271
560 Broadway
suite 307
New York, NY 10012
p (212) 219-0082
f (212) 219-0699
www.sukadesign.com

SVP Partners
page 259
15 cannon Road
wilton, CT 06897
p (203) 761-0397
f (203) 761-0482

The works Design communication Ltd.
page 252
401 Richmond street west
suite 350
Toronto, ontario M5V 3A8 canada
p (416) 599-9991
f (416) 599-0449
www.worksdesign.com

ThinkDesign Group
page 273
514 North 3rd street
suite 201
Minneapolis, MN 55401
p (612) 338-3226
f (612) 338-3452
www.thinkdg.com

Thinkhouse creative
page 290
3500 Piedmont Road, #210
Atlanta, GA 30305
p (404) 233-9850
f (404) 240-0284
www.thinkhouse.com

Turner & Associates
pages 176-177,195,241,265,299
487 Bryant street
2nd floor
san Francisco, CA 94107
p (415) 344-0990
f (415) 344-0991
www.turnersf.com

VSA Partners
pages 192,219,229,257,
267,273-275,297
1347 south state street
chicago, IL 60605
p (312) 427-6413
f (312) 427-3246
www.vsapartners.com

weymouth Design
pages 196,230,242,265,276
332 congress street
6th floor
Boston, MA 02210
p (617) 542-2647
f (617) 451-6233
www.weymouthdesign.com

weymouth Design
page 284
600 Townsend street
suite 320E
san Francisco, CA 94103
p (415) 487-7900
f (415) 431-7200
www.weymouthdesign.com

brian adams
page 300
1961 aloma avenue #154
winter park, FL 32792
p (813) 431-4202

Thomas Michael Alleman
pages 26-27
4315 avocado street, #3
Los angeles, CA 90027
p (323) 906-0460
p (310) 963-0358
f (323) 906-0464

Tony Armour photography Inc.
page 258
1726 North clybourn avenue
chicago, IL 60614
p (312) 266-1662
f (312) 266-8693
tony@tonyarmour.com

john arsenault
page 270
535 west 23rd street
#11Q south
New York, NY 10011
p (917) 447-1001
john@ponygirl171.com

Ted Axelrod
page 111
288 claremont avenue
Montclaire, NJ 07042
p (973) 744-8780
f (973) 744-8781
ted@axelrodphotography.com
www.axelrodphotography.com

chris ayers
pages 66-67
2510 old Middlefield way, unit I
Mountain view, CA 94043
p (650) 961-2700
p (888) 644-2700
f (650) 961-2722
chris@ayersphoto.com
www.ayersphoto.com

Dennis Ayuson
pages 256,279
1658 North Milwaukee avenue
chicago, IL 60647
p (773) 793-4901
dayuson@yahoo.com

Robert Bacall Representatives
pages 74-75
16 Penn Plaza, 17th Floor
suite 1754
New York, NY 10001
p (212) 695-1729
f (212) 695-1739
rob@bacall.com
www.bacall.com

Mark Battrell photography
page 254
1147 west ohio street
suite 302
chicago, IL 60622-6475
p (312) 829-2290
f (312) 829-2291
mark@battrell.com

Andy Bennett
pages 261,269
9108 chancellor Row, #B
Dallas, TX 75247
p (214) 637-9050
andy@abennettphoto.com
www.abennettphoto.com

Leem Jun Bin
pages 211,247,291

Tyler Boley
page 288
55 south Atlantic
seattle, WA 98134
p (206) 860-7166
f (206) 860-0174
tyler@tylerboley.com

Miles Boone photography
pages 112-113
117 second street
Downers Grove, IL 60515
p (630) 963-1667
f (630) 963-1668
miles@milesboonephotography.com
www.milesboonephotography.com

Lou Bopp
pages 24-25
NYC studio
p (212) 665-6400
Represented By: Elise caputo & Associates Ltd.
p (212) 725-0503
bopp@loubopp.com
www.loubopp.com www.elisecaputo.com

Andrew Borowiec
pages 243,271
10803 Magnolia Drive
cleveland, OH 44106
p (216) 791-7721
f (216) 791-9560

Matthew Borkoski photography
pages 56-57
912 Loxford Terrace
silver spring, MD 20901
p (301) 681-3051
f (301) 593-9582
matthew@imagescapes.com
www.imagescapes.com

Bela Borsodi
pages 172-173,201,213,249,301
647 east 11th street, #9
New York, NY 10009
p (212) 529-5958
belaborsodi@mac.com

Adrian Bradshaw
page 257
Getty Images
PO BOX 953604
st. Louis, MO 63195
p (877) 438-8966

Lorne Bridgman
pages 207,244,277
#302-146 Brock Avenue
Toronto, ontario M6K 2L4 canada
p (416) 873-5343
lorne.obscura@sympatico.ca

julian Broad
page 275
c/o Bill charles
116 elizabeth street
New York, NY 10013
p (212) 965-1465
f (212) 965-9235

keith Brofsky
pages 38-39
12525 sunrise Drive NE
Bainbridge Island, WA 98110
p (206) 842-0756
c (206) 999-5840
f (206) 842-0756
keith@brofsky.com
www.brofsky.com

craig Bromley
pages 48-49
1136 Briarcliff Road, studio Z
Atlanta, GA 30306
p (404) 881-0767
p (404) 229-7279
f (404) 881-1873
craig@cbromley.com
www.cbromley.com

Mark Bumgarner photography
pages 178-179,248,294
p (214) 634-4498

Alice Butterick
pages 80-81
10344 west Loyola Drive
Los Altos, CA 94024
p(650) 917-1155
f (650) 917-1133
alice@butterick.org
www.alicebutterickconcepts.com

Robie capps
pages 178-179,248,294
p (214) 761-9339
rcapps@swbell.net

elise caputo & associates ltd.
pages 24-25
240 east 27th street
New York, NY 10016
p (212) 725-0503
f (212) 683-4673
elise@elisecaputo.com
www.elisecaputo.com

elisa cicinelli
page 122
san francisco, CA
p (415) 775-8944
f (415) 775-8998
elisa@ciciphoto.com
www.ciciphoto.com

paul o. colliton studio
page 270
305 7th Avenue
penthouse
New York, NY 10001
p (212) 807-6192
f (212) 627-1788
paul@collitonstudio.com
info@collitonstudio.com
www.collitonstudio.com

jim coon studio
page 259
56 Arbor street
Hartford, CT 06101
p (860) 236-5262
f (860) 236-4863
shakti@htplx.net

jeff corwin
page 277
4433 47th Avenue south
seattle, WA 98118
p (206) 725-2272
f (206) 725-2272
jcpwash@earthlink.net

william coupon
pages 40-41
81 Nassau street, studio 2I
New York, NY 10038
p (212) 406-6936
c (646) 338-3844
f (212) 406-6940
wcoupon@mac.com
www.williamcoupon.com

Gabriel covian
pages 217,264
16 De septiembre #50
col. Manuel Avila camacho
53910 edo. De Mexico
p 52-939-476

Greg crawford
page 281
500 south Raymond Avenue
Pasadena, CA 91105
p (626) 395-0888
f (626) 395-0899
gregc@cmgdesign.com

craig cutler
page 263
15 east 32nd street
New York, NY 10016
p (212) 779-9755

Aida Daay
page 284
12 chonticleer street
Larkspur, CA 94939
p (415) 924-6374

Gary Darby
page 300

cameron Davidson
page 295
4633 south 36th street, #A1
Arlington, VA 22206
p (703) 845-0547
f (703) 845-9542
cameron@camerondavidson.com
www.camerondavidson.com

vincent Dixon
pages 207,244,277
c/o Friend & Johnson
137 west 14th street #204
New York, NY 10011
p (212) 337-0050

Todd Doebel
page 270
246 west 73rd street
New York, NY 10023
p (212) 595-8017
boeboe@mindspring.com

elena Dorfman
page 258

philip Dykes
pages 228,256
226 whitney Avenue
Langdon, Alberta T0J 1X1 canada
p (403) 875-5353

Andrew easson
page 261
550 Queen street east
Toronto, ontario M5A 1V2 canada
p (416) 873-8704
f (416) 367-1847
andrew@easson.com

John Paul endress
pages 205,216,253
200 Roseland Avenue
essex Falls, NJ 07021
p (973) 464-1274

steven edson photography, Inc.
pages 50-51
45 Lansing Road
west Newton, MA 02465
p (617) 527-2424
p (800) 220-9765
f(617) 527-2323
steve@stevenedson.com
www.stevenedson.com

Dwight eschliman
pages 235,245,287
2325 3rd street
san Francisco, CA 94107
p (415) 861-5916
f (415) 861-5919
dwight@eschlimanphoto.com
www.eschlimanphoto.com
www.apostrophe.net

Martin evening
page 252
20 Red square
carysfort Road
London, N16 9AB United Kingdom
p 44-207-249-1864
f 44-207-503-3445

philip Ferrari
page 120
11717 sorrento valley Road
san Diego, CA 92121
p (858) 792-8011
f (858) 481-6499
phil@ferrariproductions.com
www.ferrariproductions.com

David Fine
page 42-43
Fine Imaging, Inc.
3416 woodshire crossing
Marietta, GA 30066
p (770) 579-9062
f (770) 579-9263
david@fineimaging.com
www.fineimaging.com

wendy Fletcher
pages 199,286,293
1915 cedar Lodge Terrace
Los Angeles, CA 90039
p (323) 912-9292

Doug Fogelson
page 255
1609 North Wolcott #304
chicago, IL 60622
p (773) 395-9433

chip forelli studio
pages 98-99
HC 69 Box 348 SR 371
Damascus, PA 18415
p (877) 367-3554
photo@chipforelli.com
www.chipforelli.com

Andy Freeberg
pages 104-105
678 Northern Avenue
Mill Valley, CA 94941
p (415) 381-5585
f (415) 381-6021
af@andyfreeberg.com
www.andyfreeberg.com

Kenneth Gabrielsen
pages 28-29
29 Wolf Road
croton on Hudson, NY 10520
p (212) 741-6968
p (914) 827-3970
www.gabrielsenphotography.com

Alain Giraud
page 255
c/o shop Rico
384 Atlantic Avenue
Brooklyn, NY 11217
p (718) 797-2077

Melody George
pages 90-91
542 south second street
Bellaire, TX 77401
p (713) 661-6521
f (713) 662-9994
rlmarb@swbell.net

Getty Images
pages 102-103
75 varick street, 5th floor
New York, NY 10013
p (646) 613-3815
f (646) 613-3601
www.gettyimages.com

Thomas Gibson
page 121
2820 cherry street
Kansas city, MO 64108
p (816) 531-1312
f (816) 531-8441
thom@studio1kc.com
www.studio1kc.com

Gregg Goldman Photography
page 295
5200 shaw
st. Louis, MO 63110
p (314) 771-7227
f (314) 771-7447

Misha Gravenor
pages 282,297
c/o Deb Schwartz Reps
841 stratford Avenue
south Pasadena, CA 91030
p (626) 441-2224
f (626) 441-2225

Mark Green
page 283
1022 Wirt Road
suite 302
Houston, TX 77055
p (713) 956-7978
f (713) 956-7979
mark@mgreen.com

Joe Grisham
pages 178-179,248,294
2036 commerce
Dallas, TX 75201
p (214) 231-0991

Harleywood studio
pages 232,273
3700 West Juneau Avenue
Milwaukee, WI 53208
p (414) 343-8300

Michael Hart Photography
pages 90-91
7320 Ashcroft, suite 105
Houston, TX 77081
p (713) 271-8250
f (713) 271-6008
Represented By: Melody George
p (713) 661-6521
mhart@hartphoto.com
www.hartphoto.com

Bill Hebert
page 274
45 college Avenue SE
Grand Rapids, MI 49503
p (616) 456-5083

Todd Hido
page 252
5515 carlton street
oakland, CA 94618
p (510) 420-1849
f (510) 420-1847

Robert Houser
pages 82-83
215 san carlos Avenue
Piedmont, CA 94611
p (415) 252-7818
f (510) 595-0991
bob@roberthouser.com
www.roberthouser.com

Paul S. Howell
pages 96-97
PO Box 7874
Houston, TX 77270
p (713) 521-9865
c (713) 478-0061
pshowell@earthlink.net
www.pshowell.com

Alec Huff
pages 86-87
1101 south Humphrey
oak Park, IL 60304
p 312) 504-4885
f (708) 445-8551
alechuff@earthlink.net
www.alechuff.com

Paul Hultberg
page 290
933 Watkins street NW
suite E
Atlanta, GA 30318
p (404) 817-7055
f (404) 817-9384
paul@phpictures.com

Dana Hursey
pages 116-117
2750 Highview Avenue
Altadena, CA 91001
p (626) 345-9996
f (626) 345-9966
dana@hursey.com
www.hursey.com

David Johnson
page 123
940 4th Avenue south
Nashville, TN 37210
p (615) 255-8939
david@davidjohnsonphoto.com
www.davidjohnsonphoto.com

chad Johnston
page 254
4029 8th street SE, #122
calgary, Alberta T2A 3A5 canada
p (403) 616-5810

Peter Kao
pages 178-179,248,294
Greg Booth & Associates
9004 Ambassador Row
Dallas, TX 75247
p (214) 688-1855

Jim Karageorge
pages 36-37
7349 Lucas valley Road
Nicasio, CA 94946
p (415) 662-6940
f (415) 662-6930
photoboy@karageorgestudio.com
www.karageorgestudio.com

David Katzenstein
page 280
23 East 4th Street
New York, NY 10003
p (212) 529-9460
f (212) 995-0259

Miles Keep
page 109
Photography & Digital Imagery, Inc.
2162 Old Middlefield Way
Mountain View, CA 94043
p (650) 969-6701
f (650) 961-7633
miles@mileskeepfoto.com
www.mileskeepfoto.com

Sian Kennedy
pages 234, 283
594 Broadway, #908
New York, NY 10012
p (212) 219-1269

Chris Kirzeder
pages 194, 256, 264, 296
1609 North Wolcott
Chicago, IL 60622
p (773) 342-1176
f (773) 342-5576

Bruce Kluckhohn Photography
pages 64-65
2121 Glenhurst Road
Minneapolis, MN 55416
p (612) 929-6010
bruce@brucekphoto.com
www.brucekphoto.com

Knutson Photography, Inc.
pages 34-35
1807 Elliot Avenue South, Suite 5
Minneapolis, MN 55404
p (612) 870-7376
p (888) 870-7376
f (612) 871-6614
doug@knutsonphoto.com
www.knutsonphoto.com

Kucine Photography, Inc.
pages 88-89
273 Presumpscott Street
Portland, ME 04103
p (207) 773-2568
c (207) 650-4519
f (207) 773-2568
info@kucinephoto.com
www.kucinephoto.com

Young Lee
pages 184-185, 198, 208, 233, 262, 279
3024 59th Avenue SW, #202
Seattle, WA 98116
p (206) 262-0811

Paula Lerner
pages 60-61
30 Selwyn Road
Belmont, MA 02478
p (617) 489-6747
f (617) 489-6191
paula@lernerphoto.com
www.lernerphoto.com

Michael LoBiondo Photographic
page 114
118 East Kingston Avenue, #27
Charlotte, NC 28203
p (704) 372-2456
f (704) 333-5914
michael@mlobiondo.com
www.mlobiondo.com

Graham MacIndoe
pages 234, 283
229 Dean Street
Brooklyn, NY 11217
p (718) 243-0604
f (718) 243-0604

Majed Photographic Illustration
page 119
728 Divisadero Street
San Francisco, CA 94117
f (415) 621-2824
p (415) 928-3243
majed@majedphoto.com
www.majedphoto.com

Malone and Company
pages 188-189, 294
1412 Howard Street
Omaha, NE 68102
p (402) 344-3786

Armand Marsalis
page 257
325 Potrero Avenue, #4
San Francisco, CA 94105
p (415) 626-1959

Don Mason
page 288
80 South Jackson
Seattle, WA 98104
p (206) 624-1668
f (206) 624-1724

Todd May
page 59
May's Photography
296 B Weymouth Street
Rockland, NJ 07370
p (781) 878-5149
f (781) 878-0086
todd@maysphotography.com
www.maysphotography.com

Mary Jo McConoltay
pages 184-185, 198, 208, 233, 279

Jock McDonald Photography
pages 176-177, 195, 197, 231, 241, 265, 272, 299
301 8th Street, #205
San Francisco, CA 94103
p (415) 621-0492
f (415) 621-0601

Matthew McKee Photography
pages 94-95
16 Summer Street
Dedham, MA 02026
p (781) 329-4109
f (781) 326-5380
matt@mckeephotography.com
www.mckeephotography.com

McKenzie Photography
page 115
133 West Vermont Avenue
Southern Pines, NC 28387
p (910) 692-1712
p (877) 692-1712
f (910) 692-1714
mcfoto@pinehurst.net
www.mckenziephotography.com

Patrick McNamara
pages 74-75
17 Pine Hill Road
Cape Neddick, ME 03902
p (207) 363-8474
f (207) 363-8474
Represented By: Robert Bacall Representatives
p (212) 695-1729
patrick@patrickmcnamaraphoto.com
www.patrickmcnamaraphoto.com

Melgar Photography
pages 289
San Jose CA

Nick Merrick
page 274
c/o Hedrich Blessing
741 Camino Los Abuelos
Galisteo, NM 87540
p (505) 466-2238
f (505) 466-2268

Arthur Meyerson Photography
page 254
2710 Bissonnet Street
Houston, TX 77005
p (713) 529-9697
f (713) 529-8525
arthur@arthurmeyerson.com
www.arthurmeyerson.com

eric millette
pages 62-63
656 second avenue
san francisco, ca 94118
p (415) 750-9999
f (415) 750-0329
eric@ericmillette.com
www.ericmillette.com

eric myer
pages 240,259,266,285
5821 fox view drive
malibu, ca 90265
p (310) 589-5092
f (310) 589-5192
ericmyer@ericmyer.com
info@ericmyer.com
www.ericmyer.com

Tadd myers
pages 178-179,248,294
1027 dragon street
dallas, TX 75207
p (214) 752-2372

Robert Neumann photography
pages 92-93
312 ellsworth sw
Grand Rapids, MI 49503
p (616) 454-1001
f (616) 454-4546
rneumann@bigeventstudios.com

Dan Newlen
page 272
7038 east osborn road
scottsdale, AZ 85251
p (480) 970-1400
f (480) 429-8577

Karen Nichols
page 252
951-2 old county road, #284
Bemlont, CA 94002

Jeffrey D. Noble
pages 52-53
Noble studios, Inc.,
1425 North 1st street, #101
phoenix, AZ 85004
p (602) 440-4900
p (800) 777-6625
f (602) 440-4907
jeff@noblestock.com
www.noblestock.com

Greg O'Loughlin
page 54
31262 Brooks street
Laguna Beach, CA 92651
p (949) 212-1417
f (949) 499-2241
info@grego.com
www.grego.com

Michael Paras
pages 72-73
350 7th Avenue, suite 2205
New York, NY 10001
p (212) 736-7835
f (212) 736-0387
paras@parasphotography.com
www.parasphotography.com

Joe Pellegrini
page 258
2021 west race
chicago, IL 60612
p (312) 829-2860
f (312) 829-2861

Pelosi & chambers
pages 30-31
1422 woodmont Lane
Atlanta, GA 30318
p (404) 352-9797
f (404) 352-9773
pelosi-chambers@mindspring.com
www.pelosi-chambers.com

victor John Penner Photography Inc.
page 292
2104 east 19th Avenue
vancouver, British columbia V5N 2J4
canada
p (604) 341-2397
f (604) 434-2370
vic@pennerphoto.com vjp@telus.net
www.pennerphoto.com

pictureboy creative
page 55
1212 Jarvis Avenue
elk Grove village, IL 60007
p (847) 437-3334
f (847) 437-3359
pictureboy@interaccess.com
www.pictureboyphotography.com

Matthew Plexman
page 252
11 carlaw Avenue
unit 6
Toronto, ontario M4M 2A6 canada
p (416) 463-3914
f (416) 461-6915
matthew@plexman.com

David Plunkert
pages 225,296
3504 Ash street
Baltimore, MD 21211
p (410) 235-7803
f (410) 235-4674

Daniel Portnoy
page 77
10179 sw 127th street
Miami, FL 33176
p (305) 253-8263
daniel@danielportnoy.com

Michael Prince
pages 257,275
38A windsor place
Brooklyn, NY 11215
p (718) 415-7816
f (718) 832-7810
www.michaelprince.com

Dave Putnam
page 300

Djamel Ramoul
page 110
2860 south east 34th street
ocala, FL 34471
p (352) 425-8611
f (352) 622-9200
photo@artphotosite.com
www.artphotosite.com

Redux
page 58
116 east 16th street, 12th floor
New York, NY 10003
p (212) 253-0399
f (212) 253-0397
www.reduxpictures.com

Paul Reed
page 272

vincent J. Ricardel
page 298
p (212) 445-0715
vricardel@aol.com

Francois Robert
page 274
www.andersonhopkins.com

Liz Roll
page 118
2307 North Lexington street
Arlington, VA 22205
p (703) 532-6173
f (703) 532-2143
liz.roll@rollfilm.net
www.rollfilm.net

Len Rubenstein Photography
pages 32-33
41 ocean Avenue
North scituate, MA 02066
p (781) 545-1044
f (781) 544-3322
lenrphoto@aol.com
www.lenrubenstein.com

greg samata
page 296
101 south first street
Dundee, IL 60118
p (847) 428-4440
f (847) 428-6564
greg@noisemakerfilms.com

sandro
page 279
2540 west Huron street
chicago, IL 60612
p (773) 486-0300
f (773) 486-0635
sandro@sandrofilm.com
www.sandrofilm.com

Robert schlatter
page 300
1 clarence place
san francisco, CA 94107
p (415) 284-0830

James schnepf
pages 20-21
N34 W5543 Hamilton Road
cedarburg, WI 53012
p (262) 375-2600
f (262) 375-7226
jim@schnepfphoto.com
www.schnepfphoto.com

Robert schoen
pages 46-47
185 parker street
Acton, MA 01720
p (978) 897-3242
f (978) 897-3242
robert@schoenphoto.com
www.schoenphoto.com

carlos serrao
page 275
131 varick street
suite 913
New York, NY 10013
p (212) 677-1484

Bill sharpe
page 274
1521 woodlawn se
Grand Rapids, MI 49506
p (616) 949-5036

silver Lining Digital Inc.
page 124
5000 west Roosevelt Road
chicago, IL 60644
p (773) 287-8400
f (773) 287-3320
rep@silverlining.cc
www.silverliningdigital.com

charlie simokaitis
pages 232,273-274
2454 west Hutchinson street
chicago, IL 60618
p (773) 539-4644
f (773) 539-4626

keith skelton
pages 70-71,288
Los Angeles, CA
p (213) 804-1116
www.keithskelton.com

justin smith photography
page 108
1010 east powhatan Avenue
Tampa, FL 33604
p (813) 236-7797
f (813) 236-7797
justin@justinsmith.biz
www.justinsmith.biz

Gerardo somoza
pages 78-79
247 west 30th street
New York, NY 10001
p (212) 868-0612
f (212) 868-2818
gerardophoto@mindspring.com
www.gerardophoto.com

jonathan sprague
page 58
115 san jose Avenue #2
san francisco, CA 94110
p (415) 401-7071
f (415) 401-7072
jonathansprague@mindspring.com
www.jonathansprague.com

clay stang
pages 180-181,204,253
calgary Alberta T2M 1S9 canada
p (403) 708-1434

eric staudenmaier
pages 205,216,253
919 Indiana Avenue
south pasadena, CA 91030
p (626) 403-0914

john still
page 127
still, Inc.
14 Maple park
Newton, MA 02459
p (617) 527-9911
p (866) 684-4366
f (617) 527-9912
info@johnstill.com
www.johnstill.com

jamey stillings
page 277
83 placita de oro
studio 7
santa fe, NM 87501
p (505) 984-9999
f (505) 984-9997
jamey@jstillings.com
www.jameystillings.com

matt stuart
pages 174-175,209,282
44A st. peters street
London, N1 8JT england

Maja swannie
page 297
108, 1215 13th street se
calgary, Alberta T2G 3J4 canada
p (403) 626-9767
f (403) 233-7374

jared sych
pages 206,260
p (403) 703-6780

jaime Tanaka
page 45
pier 70, Noonan Building #312
san francisco, CA 94107
p (415) 648-1122
c (415) 609-7000
f (415) 864-1122
jamietanada@earthlink.net
www.jamietanaka.com

jason Todd
page 44
187 east 4th street, studio 6L
New York, NY 10009
p (917) 407-6496
jasontoddphoto@mac.com
www.jasontoddphoto.com

phil Toledano
page 255
131 varick street, #1006
New York, NY 10013
p (212) 414-1622
www.ptoledano.com

Treleven photography
pages 100-101
18 North 4th street, suite 401
Minneapolis, MN 55401
p (612) 331-5305
f (612) 333-7521
joe@trelevenphotography.com
www.trelevenphotography.com

roger tully
pages 106-107
tully photo
599 fifth street
brooklyn, NY 11215
p (718) 768-7575
f (718) 768-7545
roger@tullyphoto.com
www.tullyphoto.com

marty umans
pages 68-69
29 east 19th street, 3rd floor
new york, NY 10003
p (212) 995-0100
f (212) 529-3801
marty@humansbyumans.com

steven underwood
page 252
21 merlin street
san francisco, CA 94107
p (415) 896-6486
f (415) 896-2349

theresa vargo
page 278
469 miller avenue
mill valley, CA 94941
p (415) 388-9210
vargophoto@earthlink.net

terry vine photography
page 283
2417 bartlett street
houston, TX 77098
p (713) 528-6788
f (713) 528-6852
studio@tvine.com
terry@tvine.com
www.terryvine.com

donald waller
page 76
new york, NY
p 212) 242-0030
p (201) 659-8606

james warych
page 274
3023 west lake street
niles, IL 60714
p (847) 581-0786

charlie westerman
pages 268,270
680 N lake shore drive #1412
chicago, IL 60611
p (312) 664-5837
f (312) 664-5838
charlie@charliewesterman.com

anna weymouth
page 284
3038 lyon street
san francisco, CA 94123
p (415) 867-4042

michael weymouth
pages 196,230,242,265,276
332 congress street
6th floor
boston, MA 02210
p (617) 542-2647
f (617) 451-6233

chris whalen
pages 178-179,248,294
PHONE (214) 320-3637
cwhalenphoto@hotmail.com

everard williams, jr.
page 295
746 east deodora drive
altadena, CA 91011
p (626) 296-1966
f (626) 296-1689
ewilliams@artcenter.edu

leslie williamson
page 295
920 bay street, #5
san francisco, CA 94109
p (415) 377-7200
f (415) 776-6095

dan winters
page 275
11594 otsego street
north hollywood, CA 91601
p (323) 957-5699
f (323) 957-5633

christian witkin
page 275
art department
48 green street
new york, NY 10013
p (212) 925-4222
f (212) 925-4422
www.art-dept.com

scott witte photography
pages 22-23
3025 west highland boulevard
milwaukee, WI 53208
p (414) 345-9660
p (800) 510-1930
scott@scottwitte.com
www.scottwitte.com

les wollam
pages 84-85
5215 goodwin avenue
dallas, TX 75206
p (214) 760-7721
les@leswollamphoto.com
www.leswollamphoto.com

john wong photography
pages 178-179,248,294
2039 farrington
dallas, TX 75207
p (214) 675-7808

ashton worthington
pages 211,247,291
315 west 39th street
new york, NY 10018
p (212) 564-5570
f (212) 643-9748
ashton@ashtonography.com
www.ashtonography.com

angela wyant
pages 195,241,265
641 el dorado way
sacramento, CA 95819
p (916) 731-8737

kingmond young
page 284
416 cortland avenue
san francisco, CA 94110
p (415) 206-1680
f (415) 206-1605
kingmond@sirius.com
www.kingmond.com

gerrard yunker
pages 228,256
425 105 8th avenue NW
calgary, alberta T2N 4N7 canada
p (403) 269-8345

jim ziv
page 285
3443-45 north racine avenue
chicago, IL 60657
p (773) 248-3686

christopher zsarnay
page 260
5600 everglades street
suite A
ventura, CA 93003
p (805) 644-5554
f (805) 644-0531

ILLUSTRATION

Nicky Ackland-Snow
page 129
c/o Wanda Nowak Agency
231 East 76th Street
Suite 5D
New York, NY 10021
Represented By: Wanda Nowak
p (212) 535-0438
f (212) 535-1624
wandanowak@aol.com
www.wandanow.com

American Artists
page 140
353 West 53th Street, #1W
New York, NY 10019
p (212) 682-2462
f (212) 582-0090
info@aareps.com
www.aareps.com

Neil Armstrong
pages 205,216,253
10 Rue Frechette
Longuquil, Quebec J4J 1G5 canada
p (450) 670-0895
f (450) 670-0895

Istvan Banyai
pages 219,267
PO Box 329
Lakeville, CT 06039
p (860) 435-2940
ibanyai@sbcglobal.net
www.ist-one.com

Michelle Barnes
page 134
Represented By:
David Goldman Agency
p (212) 807-6627
www.davidgoldmanagency.com
www.michellebarnes.com

Charlie Bartlett
page 288
1218 Third Avenue
Suite 620
Seattle, WA 98101
p (206) 624-0051
f (206) 624-0875

Norm Bendell
page 135
Represented By:
David Goldman Agency
p (212) 807-6627
www.davidgoldmanagency.com
www.bendellstudio.com

Frederique Bertrand
page 129
c/o Wanda Nowak Agency
231 East 76th Street
Suite 5D
New York, NY 10021
Represented By: Wanda Nowak
p (212) 535-0438 f (212) 535-1624
wandanowak@aol.com
www.wandanow.com

Brenda Brown
pages 220,268
177 South Ridgedale Avenue
East Hanover, NJ 07936
p (973) 884-9373
f (973) 428-8586

Laurent Cilluffo
page 128
c/o Wanda Nowak Agency
231 East 76th Street
Suite 5D
New York, NY 10021
Represented By: Wanda Nowak
p (212) 535-0438 f (212) 535-1624
wandanowak@aol.com
www.wandanow.com

Tavis Coburn
pages 205,216,253
63 Hemingway Crest
Markham, Ontario L3R 2S4 canada
p (416) 624-0200
tavis_coburn@mac.com
www.taviscoburn.com

David Goldman Agency
pages 132-137
41 Union Square West
Suite 918
New York, NY 10003
p (212) 807-6627
f (212) 463-8175
www.davidgoldmanagency.com

Deutsch, Inc.
page 252
5454 Beethoven Street
Los Angeles, CA 90066
p (310) 862-3000

Steve Dininno
page 133
Represented By: David Goldman Agency
p (212) 807-6627
www.davidgoldmanagency.com
www.stevedininno.com

Elli Evertsen
pages 218,266
1115 19th Street, #3
Santa Monica, CA 90403
p (310) 828-3865

Carol Fabricatore
pages 218,266
126 Holbrook Lane
Briar Cliff Manor, NY 10510
p (914) 762-0376

Nick Fasciano
pages 205,216,253

Peter Horjus
pages 217,264
3647 India Street #1
San Diego, CA 92103
p (619) 299-0729
f (619) 574-7774
horjus@cts.com

John Jinks
page 252
20 Three Mile Harbor Road/HC
East Hampton, NY 11937
john@jjinks.com
www.jjinks.com

Stephane Jorisch
page 128
c/o Wanda Nowak Agency
231 East 76th Street
Suite 5D
New York, NY 10021
Represented By: Wanda Nowak
p (212) 535-0438 f (212) 535-1624
wandanowak@aol.com
www.wandanow.com

Peter Kramer
pages 205,216,253
Lindemannstr 31
D-4023 Dusseldorf Germany
p 49-211-210-8087
f 49 211 228-541

Emmanuel Kerner
page 128
c/o Wanda Nowak Agency
231 East 76th Street
Suite 5D
New York, NY 10021
Represented By: Wanda Nowak
p (212) 535-0438 f (212) 535-1624
wandanowak@aol.com
www.wandanow.com

Koralik Associates
page 140
343 Rocky Hill Road
Galena, IL 61036
p (815) 777-0420
f (815) 777-0488
connie@koralikassoc.com
www.koralikassoc.com

Boris Kulikov
page 129
c/o Wanda Nowak Agency
231 East 76th Street
suite 5D
New York, NY 10021
Represented By: Wanda Nowak
p (212) 535-0438 f (212) 535-1624
wandanowak@aol.com
www.wandanow.com

Marie Lafrance
page 129
c/o Wanda Nowak Agency
231 East 76th Street
suite 5D
New York, NY 10021
Represented By: Wanda Nowak
p (212) 535-0438 f (212) 535-1624
wandanowak@aol.com
www.wandanow.com

Olivier Latyk
page 128
c/o Wanda Nowak Agency
231 East 76th Street
suite 5D
New York, NY 10021
Represented By: Wanda Nowak
p (212) 535-0438 f (212) 535-1624
wandanowak@aol.com
www.wandanow.com

Benoit Laverdiere
page 128
c/o Wanda Nowak Agency
231 East 76th Street
suite 5D
New York, NY 10021
Represented By: Wanda Nowak
p (212) 535-0438 f (212) 535-1624
wandanowak@aol.com
www.wandanow.com

Javier Leguizamo
page 277
2525 Main Street
suite 204
Santa Monica, CA 90405
p (310) 396-7724
f (310) 396-1686

Keith Leinweber
pages 182-183, 221, 276
601-289 Alexander Street
Vancouver, British Columbia V6A 4H6
Canada
p (604) 684-6060
f (604) 684-4274
EMAIL keith@samatamason.com

Jerome Lenz
page 254
311 West Superior Street
suite 504
Chicago, IL 60610
p (312) 337-4674
f (312) 337-3687

David Lesh
page 299
1761 Resort Road
Burt Lake, MI 49717
p (317) 253-3141
f (317) 255-8462
boardwalk@iquest.net
www.davidlesh.com

Luba Lukova
pages 223, 236, 287
p (718) 956-1045

Martin Matje
page 129
c/o Wanda Nowak Agency
231 East 76th Street
suite 5D
New York, NY 10021
Represented By: Wanda Nowak
p (212) 535-0438 f (212) 535-1624
wandanowak@aol.com
www.wandanow.com

Michael Meister
page 129
c/o Wanda Nowak Agency
231 East 76th Street
suite 5D
New York, NY 10021
Represented By: Wanda Nowak
p (212) 535-0438 f (212) 535-1624
wandanowak@aol.com
www.wandanow.com
www.michaelmeister.com

Lloyd Miller
page 143
619 East 5th Street, Apt 11
New York, NY 10009
p (212) 505-5767
f (212) 387-9694
lmillerny@aol.com
www.millerillustration.com

Michael Morgenstern
pages 130-131
8104 Marshall Avenue
Margate, NJ 08402
p (609) 823-2420
f (609) 823-2252
mmorgenstern@earthlink.net
www.mmorgenstern.com

Douglas Mullen
page 128
c/o Wanda Nowak Agency
231 East 76th Street
suite 5D
New York, NY 10021
Represented By: Wanda Nowak
p (212) 535-0438 f (212) 535-1624
wandanowak@aol.com
www.wandanow.com

Greg Newbold
page 139
3724 South 2700 East
Salt Lake City, UT 84109
p (801) 274-2407
f (801) 274-2407
greg@gregnewbold.com
www.gregnewbold.com

Wanda Nowak Agency
pages 128-129
231 East 76th Street
suite 5D
New York, NY 10021
p (212) 535-0438
f (212) 535-1624
wandanowak@aol.com
www.wandanow.com

The Orphanage
page 252
30 Mesa Street, Suite 201
San Francisco, CA 94129
p (310) 561-2570
f (415) 561-2575

David Plunkert
pages 225, 296
3504 Ash Street
Baltimore, MD 21211-1815
p (410) 235-7803
f (410) 235-4674
dave@spurdesign.com
www.spurdesign.com

Pierre Pratt
page 128
c/o Wanda Nowak Agency
231 East 76th Street
suite 5D
New York, NY 10021
Represented By: Wanda Nowak
p (212) 535-0438 f (212) 535-1624
wandanowak@aol.com
www.wandanow.com

Gavin Reece
pages 222, 281
Digital Vision
New York, NY 10016
p (212) 229-6779
f (212) 229-6821

aaron charles ahymes
page 142
1304 Black oak court
pinole, CA 94564
p (510) 724-0464
p (510) 367-3413
animecido32@yahoo.com
www.acillustrations.com

jill Rizzo
pages 188-189,294
1207 south 75th street
omaha, NE 68124
p (402) 398-1108
f (402) 398-1492

Tim Robinson
page 128
c/o wanda Nowak Agency
231 east 76th street
suite 5D, New York, NY 10021
Represented By: wanda Nowak
p (212) 535-0438 f (212) 535-1624
wandanowak@aol.com
www.wandanow.com

peter saville
page 252
1 sailmakers House
136 Narrow street
London, E14 8BP England
p 44-207-538-3001
f 44-207-513-2822

jennifer sheldon
page 138
791 Tremont street
Apartment 511 east
Boston, MA 02118
p (646) 567-8164
jennifer_sheldon@yahoo.com
www.portfolio.com/sheldon

Roger spears
pages 205,216,253
PO BOX 12037
Research Triangle park, NC 27709
p (919) 941-9000

Matthew strauss
page 136
Represented By:
David Goldman Agency
p (212) 807-6627
www.davidgoldmanagency.com
www.mstrauss.com

pepper Tharp
page 141
3718 Glendale Terrace
Minneapolis, MN 55410
p (612) 976-8383
f (612) 926 2522
peppert@visi.com
www.peppertharp.com

Liisa Turan
pages 235,245,287,300
354 pine street
san Francisco, CA 94104
p (415) 433-2035

jack unruh
pages 205,216,253
8138 santa clara
Dallas, TX 75218
p (214) 327-6211
f (214) 327-1511

elene usdin
page 129
c/o wanda Nowak Agency
231 East 76th street
suite 5D
New York, NY 10021
Represented By: wanda Nowak
p (212) 535-0438 f (212) 535-1624
wandanowak@aol.com
www.wandanow.com

David vaught
pages 178-179, 248,294
7007 Twin Hills
suite 200
Dallas, TX 75231
p (214) 987-6500

carlos vega
page 289
10803 Magnolia Drive
cleveland, OH 44106
p 216-791-7721
f 216-791-9560

Howard wakefield
page 252
1 sailmakers House
136 Narrow street
London, E14 8BP England
p 44-207-538-3001
f 44-207-513-2822

Rick wessler
page 137
Represented By: David Goldman
Agency
p (212) 807-6627
www.davidgoldmanagency.com
www.wessler3d.com

David wilcox
pages 205,216,253
1720 Holiday Lane
prescott, AZ 86305
p (928) 771-9544

Brian wong
page 271
560 Broadway
suite 307
New York, NY 10012
p (212) 219-0082
f (212) 219-0699

James Yang
page 132
Represented By: David Goldman Agency
p (212) 807-6627
www.davidgoldmanagency.com
www.jamesyang.com

Ning Yeh
page 300
21522 surveyor circle
Huntington Beach, CA 92646
p (714) 969-4470
f (714) 969-5897

Michael zaharuk
page 128
c/o wanda Nowak Agency
231 East 76th street
suite 5D
New York, 10021
Represented By: wanda Nowak
p (212) 535-0438 f (212) 535-1624
wandanowak@aol.com
www.wandanow.com

Andy zito
page 140
135 south La Brea Avenue
Los Angeles, CA 90036
p (323) 931-1182
f (323) 931-3091
Represented By: American Artists
p (212) 682-2462
Represented By: Koralik Associates
p (815) 777-0420
andyzito@hotmail.com

PRINTERS

active graphics, inc.
page 285
1532 west fulton street
chicago, IL 60607
p (312) 733-4343
f (312) 733-4614

advance printing
pages 225,296
6836 harford road
baltimore, MD 21234
p (410) 254-1111
FAX (410) 426-1462

anderson lithograph
pages 176-177,197,231,234,237,252,
255,257,272,280,283-284,293,299
560 forbes boulevard
south san francisco, CA 94080
p (650) 737-3577
f (650) 737-5660

anderson lithograph
pages 218,266,274-275
3217 south garfield avenue
los angeles, CA 90040
p (800) 727-5846
f (323)722-2328

andrews connecticut
page 162
151 red stone road
manchester, CT 06040
p (860) 649-5570
f (860) 649-7800

blanchette press
pages 182-183,194,221,228,256,264,
266,276,279,285,288,292,296-297
8000 river road
richmond, british columbia v6x
1x7 canada
p (604) 270-9421
f (604) 270-3154

bruce offset
page 162
1099 greenleaf avenue
elk grove village, IL 60007
p (847) 593-5290
f (847) 593-0815

bruce printing
page 273
315 27th avenue se
minneapolis, MN 55414
p (612) 617-1353
f (612) 331-3357

calgary colorpress
pages 206,260
1145 65 avenue NE
calgary alberta T2E 8T9 canada
p (403) 516-6407
f (403) 730-4799

colorgraphics, inc.
pages 186-187,199,210,246,255,
286,291,293
14382 chambers road
tustin, CA 92780
p (949) 583-7171
f (714) 368-5812

colorgraphics, inc.
pages 158,205,216,222,253,281
150 north meyers street
los angeles, CA 90033
p (323) 261-7171
f (323) 526-2441

colorgraphics, inc.
pages 235,245,258,284,287
888 tennessee street
san francisco, CA 94107
p (415) 821-7171
f (415) 282-4557

colorgraphics, seattle
pages 184-185,198,208,233,
262,279,282,292
1421 south dean street
seattle, WA 98144
p (206) 682-7171
f (206) 329-2017

conceptual litho reproductions
page 271
418 west 25th street
new york, NY 10001
p (212) 422-2525
f (212) 206-1287

consolidated carqueville
page 268
1536 bourdon parkway
streamwood, IL 60107
p (630) 837-4500
f (630) 837-7691

coral color
page 278
50 mall drive
commack, NY 11725
p (631) 543-5200

digital color concepts
page 270
175 route 46 west
fairfield, NJ 07004
p (973) 227-2665

finlay printing
page 298
44 tobey road
bloomfield, CT 06002
p (860) 242-2800
f (860) 286-0181

fong & fong printers
page 289
3009 65th street
sacramento, CA 95820
p (800) 992-1313
f (916) 739-0350
cfong@fongprinters.com

fortran printing, inc.
pages 243,271,289
5777 grant avenue
cleveland, OH 44105
p (216) 341-1000
f (216) 341-0534

fulmar colour printing
pages 174-175,209,282
the orion centre
108 beddington lane
croudon surrey CR0 4YY england
p 44-208-688-7500

GAC
pages 288,300
2000 NW wilson street
portland, OR 97209
p (425) 391-2371
f (206) 284-3903

graphic arts center
page 295
2000 NW wilson street
portland, OR 97209
p (503) 224-7777
f (503) 222-0735

graphic press
page 300
6100 south malt avenue
commerce, CA 90040
p (323) 726-6100
f (323) 722-1877

hennegan corporation
pages 219,267
7455 empire drive
florence, KY 41042
p (800) 453-3523
f (859) 282-3602

hillside printing
page 162
4600 west roosevelt road
hillside, IL 60162
p (708) 492-4600
f (706) 449-5999

innovation printing
pages 160,207,244,277
2051 byberry road
philadelphia, PA 19116
p (800) 355-4601
p (215) 969-4600
f (215) 464-7664

JCI Graphics
page 270
10 Ocean Parkway
Suite C-2
Brooklyn, NY 11218
p (718) 633-2824
f (718) 633-8403
jcigraphics@earthlink.net

JFB & Sons Lithographers
page 280
1700 Ocean Avenue
Ronkonkoma, NY 11779
p (631) 467-1444
f (631) 467-1666

Lake County Press, Inc.
pages 159,258
98 Noll Street
Waukegan, IL 60085
p (847) 336-4333
f (847) 336-5846
www.lakecountypress.com

LB Graph-X
page 157
246 West 54th Street
Lower Level
New York, NY 10019
p (212) 543-9200
f (212) 543-2297

Lithographix
pages 262,267,276-277
13500 South Figueroa Street
Los Angeles, CA 90061-1035
p (213) 770-1000
f (213) 770-1731

Merrill/Daniels
page 259
40 Commercial Street
Everett, MA 02149
p (617) 389-7900
f (617) 389-2835

Moore Wallace Andrew
page 269
521 Fifth Avenue
20th Floor
New York, NY 10175
p (212) 681-6002
f (212) 681-6028

O'Neil Printing
page 272
366 North 2nd Avenue
Phoenix, AZ 85003
p (602) 258-7789
f (602) 258-4504

Omaha Printing
pages 188-189,294
4700 F Street
Omaha, NE 68117
p (402) 734-4400

Oscar Printing
page 278
57 Columbia Square
San Francisco, CA 94103
p (415) 626-8818
f (415) 626-8828

Padgett Printing
page 261
1313 North Industrial Boulevard
Dallas, TX 75207
p (214) 915-6319

Print International
page 286
27 St. John's Place
Freeport, NY 11520
p (516) 223-7177
f (516) 783-9317

Quantum Color Graphic
pages 217,264
6511 West Oakton Street
Morton Grove, IL 60053
p (847) 967-3600
f (847) 967-3610

Quebecor World-Acme Printing
pages 196,230,242,254,265,290
30 Industrial Way
Wilmington, MA 01887
p (978) 658-0800
f (978) 658-3202
www.quebecorworld.com

Rainbow Graphics
page 290
575 Commerce Park Drive
Marietta, GA 30060
p (770) 426-9100
f (770) 426-9312

Samsung Moonwha Printing Co.
pages 211,247,291
#278-34 2ga, Songsu
Songdong-gu, Seoul Korea
p 02-468-0361
f 02-461-6798

St. Ives Burrups
pages 192,229,257
London UK
p 44-20-8317-3976
f 44-20-8854-5927

Sandy Alexander
pages 192,229,257,263,275,297,299
200 Entin Road
Clifton, NJ 07014
p (973) 470-8100
f (973) 470-9269

Somerset Graphics Co. Ltd.
pages 223,236,252,287
370 Brunel Road
Mississauga, Ontario L4Z 2C2 Canada
p (905) 890-2553
f (905) 890-7489

Southern California Graphics
pages 260,281
8432 Stellar Drive
Culver City, CA 90232
p (310) 559-3600
f (310) 558-3127

Steketee-VanHuis, Inc.
page 274
13 West 4th Street
Holland, MI 49423
p (616) 392-2326
f (616) 392-9041
www.svhgroup.com

Sundog Printing Ltd
pages 180-181,204,206,253-254,260
1311 9th Avenue SW
Calgary, Alberta T3C 0H9 Canada
p (403) 262-0897
f (403) 294-1496

Waller Press
pages 200,212,298
339 Harbor Way
South San Francisco, CA 94080
p (650) 589-6262
f (650) 589-0578

Watermark Press
pages 195,241,265
950 Tennessee Street
San Francisco, CA 94107
p (415) 913-4619
f (415) 282-6800

W.E. Andrews
page 162
140 South Road
Bedford, MA 01730
p (781) 275 0720
f (781) 276-2494

Wetmore Printing
page 283
1645 West Sam Houston Parkway North
Houston, TX 77043
p (713) 468-7175
f (713) 468-8021

Williamson Printing
pages 178-179,240,248,259,269,294
6700 Denton Drive
Dallas, TX 75235
p (214) 404-2100

PAPER MANUFACTURERS

Appleton coated LLC
pages 200,205,212,216,234,253,
258,280,283,298
569 carter court
Kimberly, WI 54136
p (920) 968-3999
f (920) 968-3950

Bradner smith & company
page 268
2300 Arthur Avenue
Elk Grove village, IL 60007
p (847) 290-8485
f (847) 290-8486

Domtar Inc.
pages 151-152,182-183,221,
228,256,276,288
395 de Maisonneuve Boulevard west
Montreal H3A 1L6 canada
p (800) 267-2040
f (800) 267-4050

Domtar Paper
pages 220,268
9500 west Bryn Mawr Avenue
suite 300
Rosemont, IL 60018

Fiber Mark
pages 205,216,253
PO BOX 498
Brattleboro, VT 05302
p (802) 257-0365
f (802) 257-5973
info@fibermark.com

Finch Pruyn & company, Inc.
pages 184-185,198,208,225,233,
259,269,279-280,289,296
one Glen street
Glens Falls, NY 12801
p (800) 833-9981
f (518) 743-9656

Fox River Paper company
pages 195,241,257,259,265,
269,272,283
100 west Lawrence street
PO BOX 2215
Appleton, MT 59912
p (847) 777-2784
f (847) 777-2560

Fraser Paper
pages 182-183,218,221,223,228,236,
252,256,266,276,279,285,287,295-297
70 seaview Avenue, 6th Floor
PO BOX 10055
stamford, CT 06902
p (203) 705-2800
f (203) 705-2801
www.fraserpapers.com

French Paper company
pages 243,271,289
100 French street
Niles, MI 49120-2854
p (616) 683-1100
f (612) 683-3025
french@frenchpaper.com
www.frenchpaper.com

G.F. smith & son London Ltd
pages 174-175,209,282
Lockwood street
Hull, HU2 OHL England
p 1482-323-503
f 1482-223-174
info@gfsmith.com
www.gfsmith.com

Gilbert Paper company
pages 188-189,294
100 west Lawrence street
Appleton, WI 54912-1629
p (800) 445-7329
f (920) 336-7125

International Paper
pages 267,278,289,300
400 Atlantic street
stamford, CT 06921
p (800) 223-1268

Mead westvaco corporation
pages 188-189,252,266,275,294
1 High Ridge Park
stamford, CT 06905
p (206)-7400
www.meadwestvaco.com

Mohawk Paper Mills, Inc.
pages 192,195-196,205,216-217,219,
229-230,241-242,253-254,257,264-267,
270,273-275,282,284,292,297-298,300
PO BOX 497
465 saratoga street
cohoes, NY 12047
p (518) 237-1740
f (518) 237-7394
www.mohawkpaper.com

Mohawk/Lindenmeyer Munroe
pages 207,244,277
one Penn Plaza
New York, NY 10019
p (212) 564-1004
f (212) 564-0108

Monadnock Paper Mills, Inc.
pages 153,261,285,299
117 Antrim Road
Bennington, NH 03442
p (603) 588-3311
f (603) 588-3158

M-Real corporation
pages 154-155,271
100 Demarest Drive
wayne, NJ 07470
p (203) 229-7468
f (203) 229-7499

New Leaf Paper
pages 176-177,299
215 Leidesdorff street
4th Floor
san Francisco, CA 94111
p (888) 989-5323
f (415) 291-9353
www.newleafpaper.com

Nisshinbo
pages 211,247,291
2-31-11 Ningyo-cho Nihonbashi
chuo-ku, 103-8650 Tokyo Japan
p 81-3-5695-8933
f 81-3-5695-8982
spteam@nisshinbo.co.jp
www.nisshinbo.co.jp

Potlatch
page 255, 263
3100 south Harbor Boulevard
suite 180
santa Ana, CA 92704
p (714) 424-4648
f (714) 754-1805

sappi Fine Paper North America
pages 15,194,196-197,199,230-
231,237,242,260,264-265,272,276-
279,281,284,286-287,292-293,296
225 Franklin street
Boston, MA 02110
p (617) 423-7300
f (617) 423-5491
www.sappi.com

scheufelen North America
pages 220,258,268,286
187 Danbury Road
wilton, CT 06897
p (800) 220-8577

smart Paper
pages 17-18, 125-126
601 North B street
Hamilton, OH 45013
p (800) 443-973
p (513) 869-5000
f (513) 869-5062

spicers Paper
pages 222,281
12310 East slauson Avenue
santa Fe springs, CA 90670
p (562) 698-1199
f (562) 693-8339
sfs@spicers.com

stora enso North America
pages 156,252,255,290
2700 River Road
suite 210
Des Plaines, IL 60018
p (715) 422-3111
f (715) 422-3469
www.storaenso.com/na

unisource
pages 268,297
1141 North swift Road
Addison, IL 60101
p (630) 875-7000
f (630) 705-6110
www.unisourcelink.com

wausau paper mills company
page 274
1244 Kronenwetter Drive
Mosinee, WI 54455-9099
p (715) 693-4470
www.wausaumosinee.com

weyerhaeuser company
pages 149-150,178-181,186-187,197,204,210,231,237,240
246,248,253-254,259,270,272,
283,290-291,293-294,300
33663 weyerhaeuser way south
federal way, WA 98003-9777
p (253) 924-2345
f (253) 924-3332
www.weyerhaeuser.com

yupo corporation
page 252
800 Yupo court
chesapeake, VA 23320

zanders USA
page 280
100 Demarest Drive
wayne, NJ 07470
www.zandersusa.com

PUBLISHING

AVA publishing
page 161
56a chapel Road
worthing west sussex BN11 1DQ
united Kingdom
p 44-1252-541-602
p (800) 367-9692